101 Biblical Secrets for Success

Financial, Emotional, and Spiritual

by Sherwood Jansen, Esq.

Huntington House Publishers

Huntington House Publishers
P.O. Box 53788
Lafayette, Louisiana 70505

PRINTED IN THE UNITED STATES OF AMERICA

Library of Congress Card Catalog Number 108643
ISBN 1-56384-176-2

Contents

Chapter One

Jesus Christ, Esq.

In the Lord's law, a lot is mentioned about lawyers and judges.

Solomon wrote: "In the multitude of counsellors there is safety" (Prov. 11:14); "To the counsellors of peace is joy" (Ibid., 12:20); "Without counsel purposes are disappointed: but in the multitude of counsellors they are established" (Ibid., 15:22).

David's uncle, Jonathan (not King Saul's son), was a counsellor (1 Chron. 27:32). David once said to God, "Thy testimonies also are my delight and my counsellors" (Ps. 119:24). And Job wrote that God, "leadeth counsellors away spoiled, and maketh judges fools" (Job 12:17).

The Lord told Moses,

> Judges and officers shalt thou make thee in all thy gates, which the Lord thy God giveth thee, throughout thy tribes: and they shall judge the people with just judgment. Thou shalt not wrest judgment; thou shalt not respect persons, neither take a gift: for a gift doth blind the eyes of the wise, and pervert the words of the righteous. (Deut. 16:18-9)

The Lord thought so much about judges that a whole book in the Bible was dedicated to them. It is recorded, "When the Lord raised them up judges, then the Lord was with the judge, and delivered them out of the hand of their enemies all the days of the judge" (Judg. 2:18). The first woman judge mentioned in the Bible was Deborah. She "dwelt under the palm tree of Deborah between Ramah and Bethel in mount Ephraim:

and the children of Israel came up to her for judgment" (Judg. 4:5). Even the strongman, Samson (one of the heroes of old that Jerry Siegel and Joe Shuster patterned their "Superman" comic-book character after), judged Israel for twenty years (Ibid., 15:20).

David declared, "When their judges are overthrown in stony places, they shall hear my words; for they are sweet" (Ps. 141:6). And Solomon wrote, "My wisdom dwell with prudence . . . by me princes rule, and nobles, even all the judges of the earth" (Prov. 8:12, 16). Talking to Jerusalem, the Lord said, "I will restore thy judges as at the first, and thy counsellors as at the beginning: afterward thou shalt be called, The city of righteousness, the faithful city" (Isa. 1:26).

The apostle Paul's law school professor was a man named Gamaliel, who was a "doctor of the law" (Acts 5:34). Paul wrote that he had been, "brought up . . . at the feet of Gamaliel" (Ibid., 22:3). After Paul converted to Christianity, he still associated with attorneys. We know this because he wrote to Titus and asked him to, "bring Zenas the lawyer" (Titus 3:13).

When Jesus was only 12-years-old, "they found Him in the temple, sitting in the midst of the doctors [of the law], both hearing them and asking them questions" (Luke 2:46). All who heard Him, "were astonished at His understanding and answers" (Ibid., v. 47).

Eighteen years later, after Jesus officially began His ministry, Luke wrote, "And it came to pass on a certain day, as He was teaching, that there were Pharisees and doctors of the law sitting by, which were come out of every town of Galilee, and Judea, and Jerusalem: and the power of the Lord was present to heal them" (Ibid., 5:17). Later Christ commented cryptically, "Woe unto you also, ye lawyers! For ye lade men with burdens grievous to be borne, and ye yourselves touch not the burdens with one of your fingers" (Ibid., 11:46). Evidently, those lawyers weren't willing to be healed.

John wrote, "And if any man sin, we have an advocate with the Father, Jesus Christ the righteous: and He is the propitiation for our sins: and not for our's only, but also for the sins of the whole world" (1 John 2:1-2). It is interesting that the

Greek word for *advocate* is the same word used for *Comforter* in John 14:16-7, where Jesus said, "I will pray the Father, and He shall give you another Comforter, that He may abide with you for ever; even the Spirit of truth."

Alternative dispute resolution is being used more and more frequently to settle cases, yet mediation was mentioned almost two thousand years ago by the apostle Paul, who promulgated: "Now a mediator is not a mediator of one, but God is one" (Gal. 3:20); and, "For there is one God, and one mediator between God and men, the man Christ Jesus; who gave Himself a ransom for all, to be testified in due time" (1 Tim. 2:5-6).

It is significant to note that hundreds of years before Christ was born, a Jewish prophet predicted His birth and that He would be called a lawyer: "For unto us a Child is born, unto us a Son is given: and the government shall be upon His shoulder: and His name shall be called Wonderful, Counsellor, The Mighty God, The Everlasting Father, The Prince of Peace" (Isa. 9:6).

In closing, it was Joseph, a "counsellor,"* who begged Pilate for the dead body of Jesus, and then put Him into his own burial place. Thus, Jesus was laid to rest in a lawyer's tomb!

*Luke 23:50-3; Matthew 27:60

Chapter Two

Walk With the Wise

I believe there are three ways to get wisdom: (1) Ask God (James 1:5); (2) Read books filled with wisdom (Ps. 119:100); and (3) associate with wise people. Job wrote, "With the ancient is wisdom; and in length of days understanding" (Job 12:12). But no biblical writer wrote more about the accumulation of wisdom from others than Solomon, the wisest man who ever lived (1 Kings 3:12). He held forth: "A wise man will hear, and will increase learning; and a man of understanding shall attain unto wise counsels" (Prov. 1:5); "Hear instruction, and be wise, and refuse it not" (Ibid., 8:33); "Rebuke a wise man, and he will love thee. Give instruction to a wise man, and he will be yet wiser: teach a just man, and he will increase in learning" (Ibid., 9:8-9); "The way of a fool is right in his own eyes: but he that hearkeneth unto counsel is wise" (Ibid., 12:15); "With the well-advised is wisdom" (Ibid., 13:10); "The ear of the wise seeketh knowledge" (Ibid., 18:15); "Hear counsel, and receive instruction, that thou mayest be wise in thy latter end" (Ibid., 19:20); and, "Every purpose is established by counsel" (Ibid., 20:18).

The Lord is the source of all wisdom Paul promulgated: "But unto them which are called, both Jews and Greeks, Christ the power of God, and the wisdom of God" (1 Cor. 1:24). Jude joined with, "To the only wise God our Saviour, be glory and majesty, dominion and power, both now and ever" (Jude 25). That is why Christ could say, "The queen of the south [Sheba] shall rise up in the judgment with this generation, and shall condemn it: for she came from the uttermost parts of the earth to hear the wisdom of Solomon; and, behold, a greater than Solomon is here" (Matt. 12:42).

Christ told a parable of a rich man who accused his steward of wasting assets which he had put into his trust (Luke 16:1). The rich man called the steward forth to give a final accounting, because he had determined to fire him. The steward then decided on a plan which he thought would gain him favor with his employer's debtors. He wanted them to receive him into their houses after he lost his job. The steward went to each debtor and worked out a lesser sum payment as full settlement. The rich man afterwards commended the unjust steward because he had done wisely (Ibid., v. 2-8).

Then Jesus gave the purport of His parable: "The sons of this age are shrewder and more prudent and wiser in their own generation than are the sons of light. And I tell you, make friends for yourselves by means of unrighteous mammon [money], so that when it fails, they may receive and welcome you into the everlasting habitations" (Luke 16:9-10, Amplified Bible).

Solomon summed it all up into one short sentence: "He that walketh with wise men shall be wise" (Prov. 13:20).

Chapter Three

Escape Artists

One of the greatest magicians in history, Ehrich Weiss, the son of a Jewish rabbi, was born in Budapest, Hungary. He and his family moved to the United States when he was 4-years-old. Ehrich's work as a entertainer began in his youth, when he traveled as a circus trapeze performer. He then began to specialize in feats by which he could magically escape from handcuffs and other restraints. His stage name, modified from a famous French magician, later became his legal name: *Harry Houdini.*

There are over 120 references to escapes in the Bible. The first occurrence happened when Lot was kidnapped by four kings. The Bible states that, "they took Lot, Abram's brother's son, who dwelt in Sodom, and his goods, and departed. And there came one that had escaped, and told Abram the Hebrew" (Gen. 14:13-4). Abraham immediately "armed his trained servants, born in his own house, three hundred and eighteen" and rescued his nephew (Ibid., v. 14).

Later, God dispatched two angels to destroy the city where Lot lived because of its wickedness. They told him and his family, "Escape for thy life; look not behind thee, neither stay thou in all the plain; escape to the mountain, lest thou be consumed" (Ibid., 19:17).

Mosaic law (preceding by 3,000 years the beliefs of the U.S. Abolitionists in the 1800s) stated: "Thou shalt not deliver unto his master the servant which is escaped from his master unto thee: He shall dwell with thee, even among you, in that place which he shall choose in one of thy gates, where it liketh him best: thou shalt not oppress him" (Deut. 23:15-6).

David eluded danger often. When King Saul threw a javelin at him, "David fled, and escaped" (1 Sam. 19:10). Saul promptly sent men to David's home to slay him. Michal, his wife, let David down through a window, and "he went, and fled, and escaped" (Ibid., v. 12).

As he was fleeing from Saul on another occasion, David went to Achish, king of Gath, an enemy of Israel. The servants of Achish then told the king that David was the same man about which the Israelite women had sung in dances, saying, "Saul hath slain his thousands, and David his ten thousands" (1 Sam. 21:11). When David heard what the men had said, he "changed his behavior before them, and feigned himself mad in their hands" (Ibid., v. 14). Angry because his soldiers had brought an insane person into his presence, the king dismissed David, who then "departed thence, and escaped to the cave Adullam" (Ibid., 22:1).

When the Philistines fought against the people of Keilah and were robbing their threshing floors, David and his men smote the Philistines and saved the inhabitants of Keilah (Ibid., 23:1, 5). After Saul heard that David was staying in Keilah, a town that had gates and bars, the king sent his soldiers to besiege it. David and all his men then "escaped from Keilah" and abode in the wilderness (Ibid., v. 13).

It's no wonder David declaimed: "In Thee, O Lord, do I put my trust: let me never be put to confusion. Deliver me in Thy righteousness, and cause me to escape" (Ps. 71:1-2); and, "Our soul is escaped as a bird out of the snare of the fowlers: and the snare is broken, and we are escaped. Our help is in the name of the Lord, who made heaven and earth" (Ibid., 124:7-8).

Job joined with, "My bone cleaveth to my skin and to my flesh, and I am escaped with the skin of my teeth" (Job 19:20). While Solomon said sagaciously, "I find more bitter than death the woman, whose heart is snares and nets, and her hands as bands: whoso pleaseth God shall escape from her" (Eccles. 7:26).

Isaiah included: "And the remnant that is escaped of the house of Judah shall yet again take root downward, and bear fruit upward. For out of Jerusalem shall go forth a remnant, and they that escape out of Mount Zion: the zeal of the Lord of hosts shall do this" (2 Kings 19:30-1); "In that day shall the branch of the Lord be beautiful and glorious, and the fruit of the earth shall be excellent and comely for them that are escaped of Israel" (Isa. 4:2); and, "It shall come to pass in that day, that the remnant of Israel, and such as are escaped of the house of Jacob, shall no more again stay upon him that smote them; but shall stay upon the Lord, the Holy One of Israel, in truth" (Ibid., 10:20).

Jeremiah wrote, "Ye that have escaped the sword, go away, stand not still: remember the Lord afar off, and let Jerusalem come into your mind" (Jer. 51:50). Ezra wrote, "grace hath been shewed from the Lord our God, to leave us a remnant to escape, and to give us a nail in His holy place, that our God may lighten our eyes, and give us a little reviving in our bondage" (Ezra 9:8).

When Jesus told the people that no prophet is accepted in his own country, the Jewish religious leaders became enraged. The Bible records that they, "rose up, and thrust Him out of the city, and led Him unto the brow of the hill whereon their city was built, that they might cast Him down headlong. But He passing through the midst of them went His way" (Luke 4:29-30). Another time, "they sought again to take Him: but He escaped out of their hand" (John 10:39).

Paul proffered, "In Damascus the governor under Aretas the king kept the city of the Damascenes with a garrison desirous to apprehend me: and through a window in basket was I let down by the wall, and escaped his hands" (2 Cor. 11:32-3).

Another time, when Paul was sailing on a ship to Rome with other prisoners, an angel told him one night, "Fear not, Paul; thou must be brought before Caesar: and, lo, God hath given thee all them that sail with thee" (Acts 27:24). Later, when the ship was run aground and the rear part was broken with the violence of the waves, the sailors, Paul included, "escaped all safe to land" (Ibid., v. 44).

Thus, it was with confidence that Paul could convince the church at Corinth, "There hath no temptation taken you but such is common to man: but God is faithful, who will not suffer you to be tempted above that ye are able; but will with the temptation also make a way to escape, that ye may be able to bear it" (1 Cor. 10:13).

Chapter Four

A Willing Mind
Is Enough

A willing worker is a valuable asset to a company. Exodus 35:29 states that "The children of Israel brought a willing offering unto the Lord, every man and woman, whose heart made them willing to bring for all manner of work, which the Lord had commanded to be made by the hand of Moses."

Deborah and Barak sang a song together, in which were these words: "My heart is toward the governors of Israel, that offered themselves willingly among the people. Bless ye the Lord" (Judg. 5:9).

David divined, "Thy people shall be willing in the day of Thy power in the beauties of holiness from the womb of the morning: thou hast the dew of thy youth" (Ps. 110:3); and said to his firstborn, "Solomon, my son, know thou the God of thy father, and serve Him with a perfect heart and with a willing mind: for the LORD searcheth all hearts, and understandeth all the imaginations of the thoughts: if thou seek Him, He will be found of thee" (1 Chron. 28:9).

Isaiah indicated, "If ye be willing and obedient, ye shall eat the good of the land" (Isa. 1:19). The Hebrew word translated *willing* in this verse is the same Hebrew word rendered *consent* in: "My son, if sinners entice thee, consent thou not" (Prov. 1:10). Jesus Christ, who understands the nature of man completely,* said, "The spirit indeed is willing, but the flesh is weak" (Matt. 26:41).

---

*See John 2:24-5.

Paul, in referring to his own ministry, said, "If I do this thing willingly, I have a reward" (1 Cor. 8:17). In talking about the wealthy, Paul said they should "do good, that they be rich in good works, ready to distribute, willing to communicate" (1 Tim. 6:18).

Paul also put forth, "if there be first a willing mind, it is accepted according to that a man hath, and not according to that he hath not" (2 Cor. 8:12). The *New Jerusalem Bible* makes the meaning even clearer. It renders the verse: "As long as the enthusiasm is there, the basis on which it is acceptable is what someone has, not what someone does not have." To put it in a business context, bosses love willing people because what they don't know, they can always learn.

In closing, there are two things about which God is *not* willing: (1) "He doth not afflict willingly nor grieve the children of men" (Lam. 3:33); and (2) He is "not willing that any should perish" (2 Pet. 3:9).

Chapter Five

Visit God in the Hospital

How could the Lord get sick? Didn't David write, "As for God, His way is perfect"? (Ps. 18:30). And didn't Jesus, on the sermon in the mountain, say, "Be ye therefore perfect, even as your Father which is in heaven is perfect?" (Matt. 5:48). If the Master is perfect, how could He suffer with a malady?

Even if God did get sick, how would we know it? Didn't He say, "If I were hungry, I would not tell thee: for the world is Mine, and the fullness thereof" (Ps. 50:12). If God wouldn't tell us if He was hungry, would He necessarily communicate the fact if He wasn't feeling well?

Paul stood on Mars' Hill in Athens and said to the learned Greeks, "God that made the world and all things therein, seeing that He is Lord of heaven and earth, dwelleth not in temples made with hands; neither is worshipped with men's hands, as though He needed any thing, seeing He giveth to all life, and breath, and all things" (Acts 17:24-5). If God doesn't need anything, why would He need someone to visit Him if even He was ailing?

Paul also wrote, "The weakness of God is stronger than men" (1 Cor. 1:25). If it were possible that God could become weak, would that imply that He could become ill? Even if God could get sick, didn't He say, "I am the Lord that healeth thee"? (Exod. 15:26). Didn't David declare He "healeth all thy diseases" (Ps. 103:3), and that God "sent His word, and healed and delivered them from their destruction"? (Ibid., 107:20).

The Lord asked Abraham, "Is anything too hard for the Lord?" (Gen. 18:14). Jeremiah exclaimed, "Ah Lord God! Behold, Thou hast made the heaven and the earth by Thy great power and stretched out arm, and there is nothing too hard for Thee" (Jer. 32:17). Ten verses later, the Lord reaffirmed, "Behold, I am the Lord, the God of all flesh: is there any thing too hard for Me?" If nothing is too hard for the Lord, couldn't He heal Himself if He was infirm?

Is all this discussion just counterproductive conjecture, spectral supposition, absurd assumption, nonsensical notion, or preposterous presumption? No. For Jesus said these words:

> When the Son of Man shall come in His glory, and all the holy angels with Him, then shall He sit upon the throne of His glory:
>
> Then shall the king say unto them on His right hand, "Come, ye blessed of My Father, inherit the kingdom prepared for you from the foundation of the world: For I was an hungred, and ye gave Me meat: I was thirsty, and ye gave Me drink: I was a stranger, and ye took Me in: naked, and ye clothed Me: I was sick, and ye visited Me: I was in prison and ye came unto Me."
>
> Then shall the righteous answer Him, saying, "Lord, when saw we Thee an hungred, and fed Thee? Or thirsty, and gave Thee drink? When saw we Thee sick, or in prison and came unto Thee?" And the King shall answer and say unto them, "Verily I say unto you, inasmuch as ye have done it unto one of the least of these My brethren, ye have done it unto Me." (Matt. 25:31, 34-40)

The impact of Christ's words is startling. If we do acts of kindness to the least of the brethren in our own churches, or for members of the Body of Christ at large, it is as though we did it unto the Lord Himself! The Greek word translated "least" in the verses above is the Greek word *mikros,* from where we get our English words: *micro*be, *micro*chip, *micro*fiche, *micro*film.

Chapter Six

Pour Your Passion Into It

After the Lord used Paul to heal a man who was crippled, the people who witnessed the event began calling Paul, Mercurius, and his traveling companion Barnabas, Jupiter. When the priest of Jupiter brought oxen and garlands to sacrifice to the two ministers, Paul ran amongst the people shouting, "Sirs, why do you do these things? We also are men of like passions with you, and preach unto you that ye should turn from these vanities unto the living God, which made heaven and earth, and the sea, and all things that are therein" (Acts 14:15).

Luke wrote that Jesus Christ, "shewed Himself alive after His passion by many infallible proofs, being seen of them forty days, and speaking of the things pertaining to the kingdom of God" (Ibid., 1:3).

The Greek word for "passion" used in the two verses above is *pathos,* from which we get the English words *pathetic* (arousing pity, sorrow, etc.) and *pathos* (the quality in something that arouses pity or sorrow). It is interesting to note that the Greek word for "passion" is the same word that is translated "suffer" in these selected verses:

"The members should have the same care one for another. And whether one member suffer, all the members suffer with it" (1 Cor. 12:25-6).

"For in that He Himself hath suffered being tempted, He is able to succour them that are tempted" (Heb. 2:18).

"Though He were a son, yet learned He obedience by the

things which He suffered" (Ibid., 5:8).

"For this is thankworthy, if a man for conscience toward God endure grief, suffering wrongfully" (1 Pet. 2:9).

"For it is better, if the will of God be so, that ye suffer for well doing, than for evil doing" (Ibid., 3:17).

"Wherefore let them that suffer according to the will of God commit the keeping of their souls to Him in well doing, as unto a faithful Creator" (Ibid., 4:29).

"But the God of all grace, who hath called us unto His eternal glory by Christ Jesus, after that ye have suffered a while, make you perfect, stablish, strengthen, settle you" (Ibid., 5:10).

It is interesting that the Greek word *pathos* is translated "vexed" only one time. A man brought his son to Jesus and said, "Lord, have mercy on my son: for he is lunatic, and sore vexed: for ofttimes he falleth into the fire, and oft into the water. And I brought him to Thy disciples, and they could not cure him" (Matt. 17:15).

Finally, James wrote, "The effectual,* fervent,** prayer of a righteous man availeth much. Elias was a man subject to like passions as we are, and he prayed earnestly that it might not rain: and it rained not on the earth by the space of three years and six months. And he prayed again, and the heaven gave rain, and the earth brought forth her fruit" (James 5:16-8).

Instead of feeling sorry for ourselves or wanting people to pity us, we need to pour out our passions into our destinies.

---

*Greek: *energeo,* from where we get the English word "energetic."
**Greek: *zelos,* from where we get the English word "zealous."

Chapter Seven

A Curse Without a Cause

There are a lot of Scriptures dealing with curses—almost two hundred of them. After the Flood was over and all the animals had exited the ark, Noah built an altar and sacrificed to the Lord. When God smelled the sweet savor of the barbecued meat, He said in His heart, "I will not again curse the ground any more for man's sake" (Gen. 8:21). Later, the Lord told Abraham, "I will bless them that bless thee, and curse them that curse thee" (Ibid., 12:3).

Moses, without question an expert witness on the subject of curses, chronicled these commandments of the Lord: "Thou shalt not revile the gods, nor curse the ruler of thy people" (Exod. 22:28); and "Thou shalt not curse the deaf, nor put a stumbling block before the blind, but shalt fear thy God" (Lev. 19:14).

In the book of Deuteronomy, Moses told the Levites to say these laws unto all the men of Israel with a loud voice: "Cursed be he that setteth light by his father or his mother" (Deut. 27:16); "Cursed be he that removeth his neighbor's landmark" (Ibid., v. 17); "Cursed be he that maketh the blind to wander out of the way" (Ibid., v. 18); "Cursed be he that perverteth the judgment of the stranger, fatherless, and widow" (Ibid., v. 19); "Cursed be he that smiteth his neighbour secretly" (Ibid., v. 24); and "Cursed be he that taketh reward to slay an innocent person" (Ibid., v. 25). Moses listed several dozen more curses in Deuteronomy 28:16-44, and then explained to the Israelites that, "the Lord thy God will put all these curses upon thine enemies, and on them that hate thee, which persecuted thee" (Ibid., 30:7).

Job was such man of integrity that, in referring to a man who had hated him he said, "Neither have I suffered my mouth to sin by wishing a curse to his soul" (Job 31:30). Solomon said: "He that withholdeth corn, the people shall curse him" (Prov. 11:26); "Whoso curseth his father or his mother, his lamp shall be put out in obscure darkness" (Ibid., 20:20); "He that giveth unto the poor shall not lack: but he that hideth his eyes shall have many a curse" (Ibid., 28:27); and "Accuse not a servant unto his master, lest he curse thee, and thou be found guilty" (Ibid., 30:10).

The Lord laid out to Jeremiah: "Cursed be the man that trusteth in man, and maketh flesh his arm"; and, "Cursed be he that doeth the work of the Lord deceitfully" (Ibid., 48:10). To Zechariah the Lord said, "And it shall come to pass, that as ye were a curse among the heathen, O house of Judah, and house of Israel; so will I save you, and ye shall be a blessing" (Zech. 8:13).

Jesus joined with, "Ye have heard that it hath been said, Thou shalt love thy neighbour, and hate thine enemy. But I say unto you, love your enemies, bless them that curse you, do good to them that hate you, and pray for them which despitefully use you, and persecute you" (Matt. 5:43-44).

Paul penned, "Christ hath redeemed us from the curse of the law, being made a curse for us: for it is written, 'Cursed is every one that hangeth on a tree' " (Gal. 3:13). Whereas James wrote, "Therewith bless we God, even the Father; and therewith curse we men, which are made after the similitude of God. Out of the same mouth proceedeth blessing and cursing. My brethren, these things ought not so to be" (James 3:9-10).

Moses marked, "When a prophet speaketh in the name of the Lord, if the thing follow not, nor come to pass, that is the thing which the Lord hath not spoken, but the prophet hath spoken it presumptuously: thou shalt not be afraid of him" (Deut. 18:22). In the same vein, Solomon soothed, "As the bird by wandering, as the swallow by flying, so the curse causeless shall not come" (Prov. 26:2).

Chapter Eight

Solving Sleeplessness

While Jacob was explaining to his father-in-law, Laban, that he had always worked hard for him (even though Laban had changed Jacob's wages ten times), he said,

> This twenty years have I been with thee; thy ewes and thy she goats have not cast their young, and the rams of thy flock have I not eaten. That which was torn of beasts I brought not unto thee; I bare the loss of it; of my hand didst thou require it, whether stolen by day, or stolen by night. Thus I was; in the day the drought consumed me, and the frost by night; and my sleep departed from mine eyes. (Gen. 31:40-41)

Solomon, who could speak from personal experience because he was a rich man, noted that, "the abundance of the rich will not suffer him to sleep" (Eccles. 5:12). King Darius knew he had been manipulated by his princes to throw an innocent man, Daniel, into a den of lions to face certain death. The Bible states that, "the king went to his palace, and passed the night fasting: neither were instruments of music brought before him: and his sleep went from him" (Dan. 6:18).

Because the Lord was planning to promote a certain Jew, Mordecai, He gave the king of the realm an interval of insomnia. The book of Esther records that, "On that night could not the king sleep, and he commanded to bring the book of records of the chronicles" (Esther 6:1). It was in them the king learned that Mordecai had discovered that two men had conspired to kill the king. Mordecai had alerted palace officials of the plot, which was subsequently thwarted. After reading these facts in the chronicles, the king gave honor and dignity to Mordecai.

The Bible mentions several methods to remedy bouts of insomnia. David declared: "I will both lay me down in peace, and sleep: for Thou, Lord, only makest me dwell in safety" (Ps. 4:8); and, "He giveth His beloved sleep" (Ibid., 127:2).

Solomon stated: "Keep sound wisdom and discretion: so shall they be life unto thy soul, and grace to thy neck. Then shalt thou walk in thy way safely, and thy foot shall not stumble. When thou liest down, thou shalt not be afraid: yea, thou shalt lie down, and thy sleep shall be sweet" (Prov. 3:21:24); and, "The sleep of a laboring man is sweet" (Ibid., 5:12).

The Lord prophesied that one day He would set up one Shepherd over His people. He told Ezekiel, "I will make with them a covenant of peace, and will cause the evil beasts to cease out of the land: and they shall dwell safely in the wilderness, and sleep in the woods" (Ezek. 34:25).

Since, "He that keepeth Israel shall neither slumber nor sleep" (Ps. 121:4), we can rest in peace because He watches over us.

Chapter Nine

The Original Godfather

Nowhere in the Bible is the word "motherless" mentioned, but forty-five times the word "fatherless" is used. The first instance is Exodus 22:22, which states: "Ye shall not afflict any widow, or fatherless child." Other references to the fatherless include:

"Thou shalt not pervert the judgment of the stranger, nor of the fatherless; nor take a widow's raiment to pledge: but thou shalt remember that thou wast a bondman in Egypt, and the Lord thy God redeemed thee thence" (Exod., 24:17-18);

"When thou cuttest down thine harvest in the field, and hast forgot a sheaf in the field, thou shalt not go again to fetch it: it shall be for the stranger, for the fatherless, and for the widow: that the Lord thy God may bless thee in all the work of thine hands" (Ibid., 24:19);

"For the Lord your God is God of gods, and Lord of lords, a great God, a mighty, and a terrible, which regardeth not persons, nor taketh reward: He doth execute the judgment of the fatherless and widow, and loveth the stranger, in giving him food and raiment" (Deut. 10:17-8);

"The Lord preserveth the strangers; He relieveth the fatherless and widow" (Ps. 146:9); "Thou art the helper of the fatherless" (Ibid., 10:14); "Remove not the old landmark; and enter not into the fields of the fatherless: for their Redeemer is mighty; He shall plead their cause with thee" (Prov. 23:10-1);

"Learn to do well; seek judgment, relieve the oppressed, judge the fatherless, plead for the widow" (Isa. 1:17); "If ye oppress not the stranger, the fatherless, and the widow, and shed not innocent blood in this place, neither walk after other gods to your hurt: then will I cause you to dwell in this place, in the land that I gave to your fathers, for ever and ever" (Jer. 7:6);

"Leave thy fatherless children, I will preserve them alive; and let thy widows trust in Me" (Jer. 49:11); "In thee the fatherless findeth mercy" (Hos. 14:3); and, "Pure religion and undefiled before God and the Father is this, to visit the fatherless and widows in their affliction, and to keep himself unspotted from the world" (James 1:27).

Many men, who later became famous, lost their fathers at a young age. Kit Carson's dad died when he was 9-years-old, yet Kit later became a national hero. George Washington Carver's father died when he was a child, yet he later revolutionized the economy of the South by his experiments in crop production, soil management, and various inventions. James Garfield's dad died when he was young, yet he later became the twentieth president of the U.S. As a young man, Amadaeus Gianinni saw his father shot and killed before his eyes during an argument over a small debt, yet he later founded the Bank of America. John Hancock's father died when he was a young man, yet he later was a signer of the Declaration of Independence. Paul Harvey's father died when he was 3-years-old, yet he later became the radio spokesman for middle America. Nathaniel Hawthorne's dad died when he was a child, yet he later penned the famous novel, *The Scarlet Letter*. Sam Houston's father died when he was a teenager, yet he became the president of the Republic of Texas and then a U.S. senator for fourteen years. John Johnson lost his father when he was 6-years-old, yet he later founded *Ebony* magazine. Herman Melville's father died when he was 13-years-old, yet he later wrote the famous novel, *Moby Dick*. David briefed it best when he wrote, "A Father of the fatherless, and a judge of the widows, is God in His holy habitation" (Ps. 68:5).

Chapter Ten

God Gives the Best Gifts

Everyone loves to receive gifts. The largest number of sales by commercial merchants, by far, occurs during the Christmas season because gift-giving is so prevalent. There are over 100 references to gifts and gift-giving in the Bible, including:

"Thou hast ascended on high, Thou hast led captivity captive: Thou hast received gifts for men" (Ps. 68:18); "Many will entreat the favour of the prince: and every man is a friend to him that giveth gifts" (Prov. 19:6); "Every man also to whom God hath given riches and wealth, and hath given him power to eat thereof, and to take his portion, and to rejoice in his labour; this is the gift of God" (Eccles. 5:19).

"If ye then, being evil, know how to give good gifts unto your children, how much more shall your Father which is in heaven give good things to them that ask Him?" (Matt. 7:11); "Therefore as by the offence of one judgment came upon all men to condemnation; even so by the righteousness of one the free gift came upon all men unto justification of life" (Rom. 5:18); "The gift of God is eternal life through Jesus Christ our Lord" (Rom. 6:23).

"For the gifts and calling of God are without repentance" (Ibid., 11:29); "But unto every one of us is given grace according to the measure of the gift of Christ" (Eph. 4:7); "For by grace are ye saved through faith; and that not of yourselves; it is the gift of God" (Ibid., 2:8); "Then Peter said unto them, 'Repent, and be baptized every one of you in the name of Jesus

Christ for the remission of sins, and ye shall receive the gift of the Holy Ghost' " (Acts 2:38).

But I believe the definitive Scripture regarding the subject of gifts is found in the book of James. The brother of Jesus wrote, "Every good gift and every perfect gift is from above, and cometh down from the Father of lights, with whom is no variableness, neither shadow of turning" (James 1:17). The word "lights" in this verse is the Greek word *phos*, from which comes the English word "*phos*phorus" (*light*-bearing).

Most Bible translations render "variableness" as either "no variation" or "does not change." Where it gets interesting is how different Bible versions translate the phrase "neither shadow of turning": e.g. "no shadow caused by change" (*New Jerusalem Bible*), and "or shifting shadow" (*New American Standard*).

Chapter Eleven

Count Your Joys

There are over 200 references to joy in the Bible, and almost 300 references to rejoicing. Moses mandated: "Ye shall rejoice in all you put your hand unto, ye and your households, wherein the Lord thy God hath blessed thee" (Deut. 12:7).

"Because the Lord thy God shall bless thee in all thine increase, and in all the works of thine hands, therefore thou shalt surely rejoice" (Ibid., 16:15); and, "Thou shalt rejoice in every good thing which the Lord thy God hath given unto thee, and unto thine house" (Ibid., 26:11).

Nehemiah noted, "Neither be ye sorry; for the joy of the Lord is your strength" (Neh. 8:10), while the book of Esther expressed, "The Jews had joy and gladness, a feast and a good day. And many of the people of the land became Jews" (Esther 8:17).

David wrote: "Weeping may endure for a night, but joy cometh in the morning" (Ps. 30:5); "Restore unto me the joy of Thy salvation; and uphold me with Thy free spirit" (Ibid., 51:12); "Because Thou hast been my help, therefore in the shadow of Thy wings will I rejoice" (Ibid., 63:7); "Let all those that seek Thee rejoice and be glad in Thee" (Ibid., 70:4).

"With trumpets and sound of cornet make a joyful noise before the Lord, the King" (Ibid., 98:6); "He maketh the barren woman to keep house, and to be a joyful mother of children" (Ibid., 113:9); "This is the day which the Lord hath made; we will rejoice and be glad in it" (Ibid., 117:24); "I rejoice at Thy word, as one that findeth great spoil" (Ibid., 119:162).

Solomon declared: "When it goeth well with the righteous, the city rejoiceth" (Prov. 11:10); "The heart knoweth his own bitterness; and a stranger doth not intermeddle with his joy" (Ibid., 14:10); "A man hath joy by the answer of his mouth" (Ibid., 15:23); "It is joy to the just to do judgment" (Ibid., 21:15); "When the righteous are in authority, the people rejoice" (Ibid., 29:2); "God giveth to a man that is good in His sight wisdom, and knowledge, and joy" (Eccles. 2:26); "Live joyfully with the wife whom thy lovest" (Ibid., 9:9).

Isaiah informed: "With joy shall ye draw water out of the wells of salvation" (Isa. 12:3); "The meek also shall increase their joy in the Lord" (Ibid., 9:19); "As the bridegroom rejoiceth over the bride, so shall thy God rejoice over thee" (Ibid., 62:5); "Thou meetest him that rejoiceth and worketh righteousness" (Ibid., 64:5).

Zephaniah zeroed in with, "The Lord thy God in the midst of thee is mighty; He will save, He will rejoice over thee with joy; He will rest in His love, He will joy over thee with singing" (Zeph. 3:17).

Christ confirmed: "There is joy in the presence of the angels of God over one sinner that repenteth" (Luke 15:10); and, "Ask, and ye shall receive, that your joy may be full" (John 16:24).

Paul prescribed: "Rejoicing in hope" (Rom. 12:12); "Rejoice with them that do rejoice" (Ibid., v. 15); and, "Rejoice evermore" (1 Thess. 5:16).

James did justice to this subject when he wrote, "My brethren, count it all joy when ye fall into divers temptations; knowing this, that the trying of your faith worketh patience" (James 1:2-3).

Anyone can feel joy when everything is going right. But it is much more difficult to rejoice when trials and temptations come. Instead of complaining about the situation, we need to count the previous and future joys—remember how we have successfully dealt with similar situations in the past, focus on the lessons in patience from the present predicament, and set our hopes on the happiness ahead.

Chapter Twelve

Fame Everywhere but Home

The Bible has its own list of luminaries. The social register of the Scriptures reads like this: "The Lord was with Joshua; and his fame was noised throughout all the country" (Josh. 6:27).

"Solomon's wisdom excelled the wisdom of all the children of the east country, and all the wisdom of Egypt. For he was wiser than all men; than Ethan the Ezrahite, and Heman, the Chalcol, and Darda, the sons of Mahol: and his fame was in all nations round about" (1 Kings 4:30-1).

"The fame of David went out into all lands; and the Lord brought the fear of him upon all nations" (1 Chron. 14:17); "Mordecai was great in the king's house, and his fame went out throughout all the provinces: for this man Mordecai waxed greater and greater" (Esther 9:4).

> In that day it shall be said to Jerusalem, "Fear thou not": and to Zion, "Let not thine hands be slack." Behold, at that time I will undo all that afflict thee: and I will save her that halteth, and gather her that was driven out; and I will get them praise and fame in every land where they have been put to shame. (Zeph. 3:16, 19)

In commenting about the popularity of Jesus' ministry, Luke wrote, "And the fame of Him went out into every place of the country round about" (Luke 4:37). The Greek word for "fame" in this verse is *echos* (from where we get the English word "echo"), the same Greek word that is translated "roaring" in: "There shall be signs in the sun, and in the moon, and in the stars; and upon the earth distress of nations, with perplexity; the sea and the waves roaring" (Luke 21:25); "sound" in: "And suddenly there came a sound from heaven as of a rushing mighty wind, and it filled all the house where they were sitting" (Acts 2:2); and "sounding" in: "Though I speak with tongues of men and of angels, and have not charity, I am become as sounding brass, or a tinkling cymbal" (1 Cor. 13:1).

When Jesus came back into His own country to preach, the residents there were offended at Him, saying,

> From whence hath this man these things? And what wisdom is this which is given unto Him, that even such mighty works are wrought by His hands? Is not this the carpenter, the son of Mary, the brother of James, and Joses, and of Juda, and Simon? And are not his sisters here with us? (Mark 6:2-3)

Jesus answered them and said, "A prophet is not without honor, but in his own country, and among his own kin, and in his own house" (Ibid., v. 4). The next verse then relates one of the few times that Jesus was unsuccessful in His ministry. For it states that, "He could there do no mighty work, save that He laid His hands upon a few sick folk, and healed them" (Ibid., v. 4-5).

If this happened to the Master, don't be disappointed if the same thing befalls you. Your family members, relatives, and most of your friends have probably known you for a long time. Because of their familiarity with you, they won't be in awe of your achievements. This is how it should be. Famous people need to be able to have those people around them with whom they can just "be themselves." Being continually lionized by the masses gets old after a while.

Chapter Thirteen

Have Milk?

The first time milk is mentioned in the Bible was when three angels, in the form of men, visited Abraham. He asked his unknown guests to rest themselves while he fetched them a meal. Genesis 18:8 then states that Abraham, "took butter and milk, and the calf which he had dressed, and set it before them."

The next time milk is mentioned is when Jacob called his sons together to prophesy what would happen unto them in the latter days. When Jacob got to his son Judah, he said, "The scepter shall not depart from Judah, nor a lawgiver from between his feet, until Shiloh come and unto him shall the gathering of the people be. His eyes shall be red with wine, and his teeth white with milk" (Gen., 49:12). (Maybe more milk instead of whiteners is the answer to a brighter smile!)

The phrase "land of milk and honey" is used twenty times in the Old Testament. It refers to the "Promised Land" of the Israelites. For example, Moses prayed and asked the Lord, "Look down from Thy holy habitation, from heaven, and bless Thy people Israel, and the land which Thou swarest unto our fathers, a land that floweth with milk and honey" (Deut. 26:15).

It was permissible under Mosaic law for people to sacrifice oxen, sheep, or goats to the Lord. Though the Lord allowed people to afterwards eat such animals, it was disgusting to Him to boil a young goat in its mother's milk. That's why three times the Lord specifically commanded, "Thou shalt not seethe a kid in his mother's milk."*

Job, complaining to God about his afflictions, asked, "Has Thou not poured me out as milk, and curdled me like cheese?" (Job 10:10). The prophet Agur also wrote, "Surely the churning of milk bringeth forth butter, and the wringing of the nose bringeth forth blood: so the forcing of wrath bringeth forth strife" (Prov. 30:33).

In a love song, Solomon saluted his wife, "Thy lips, O my spouse, drop as the honeycomb: honey and milk are under thy tongue; and the smell of thy garments is like the smell of Lebanon" (Song of Solomon 4:11). In romantic prose, Solomon's wife said sweetly, "His eyes are as the eyes of doves by the rivers of waters, washed with milk, and fitly set" (Ibid., 5:12).

In applying principles of memory retention, which are still valid today, Isaiah wrote,

> Whom shall He teach knowledge? And whom shall He make to understand doctrine? Them that are weaned from the milk, and drawn from the breasts. For *precept must be upon precept, precept upon precept; line upon line, line upon line; here a little, and there a little.* (Isa. 28:9-10; emphasis added)

Joel prophesied,

> The Lord also shall roar out of Zion, and utter His voice from Jerusalem; and the heavens shall shake: but the Lord will be the hope of His people, and the strength of the children of Israel. And it shall come to pass in that day, that the mountains shall drop down new wine, and the hills shall flow with milk. (Joel 3:16, 18)

Paul, in discussing how ministers should be adequately compensated, protested, "Who goeth a warfare any time at his own charges? Who planteth a vineyard, and eateth not of the fruit thereof? Or who feedeth a flock, and eateth not of the milk of the flock?" (1 Cor. 8:7).

---

*See Exodus 23:19, 34:26, and Deuteronomy 14:21.

Again, Paul, in referring to immature Christians, said, "For when for the time ye ought to be teachers, ye have need that one teach you again which be the first principles of the oracles of God; and are become such as have need of milk, and not strong meat. For every one that useth milk is unskillful in the word of righteousness: for he is a babe" (Heb. 5:12, 13). Peter concurred with Paul when he wrote, "As newborn babes, desire the sincere milk of the word, that ye may grow thereby" (1 Pet. 2:2).

The Greek word that is translated "milk" in the New Testament is *gala*. Thus, drinking the milk of God's Word should be a gala occasion.

Chapter Fourteen

Love Won't Drown

Solomon, referring to the indestructibility of love, solidified, "for love is strong as death; Many waters cannot quench love, neither can the floods drown it: if a man would give all the substance of his house for love, it would be utterly contemned [sic]" (Song of Solomon 8:6, 7).

The Pharaoh's chariots and his chosen captains were "drowned in the Red Sea" (Exod. 15:4). And those, "falsifying the balances by deceit, [who], buy the poor for silver, and the needy for a pair of shoes [shall be], cast out and drowned" (Amos 8:5, 6). Paul said that the rich can, "fall into temptation and a snare, and into many foolish and hurtful lusts, which drown men in destruction and perdition" (1 Tim. 6:9). Yet the floods can't drown love.

In referring to the toughness of love, Paul encouraged, "But let us, who are of the day, be sober, putting on the breastplate of faith and love" (1 Thess. 5:8). The Greek word translated "breastplate" is *thorax*, from which we get the English word of the same spelling, which is the part of the body between the neck and the abdomen. By implication, the word breastplate also refers to a corselet, a suit of light armor used by knights.

Paul also wrote,

> Who shall separate us from the love of Christ? Shall tribulation, or distress, or persecutions, or famine, or nakedness, or peril, or sword? . . . For I am persuaded, that neither death, nor life, nor angels, nor principali-

ties, nor powers, nor things present, nor things to come, nor height, nor depth, nor any other creature, shall be able to separate us from the love of God, which is in Christ Jesus our Lord. (Rom. 8:35, 38-39)

After Deborah and Barak led ten thousand soldiers to defeat a Canaanite king and his army, they sang a song which ended with these words: "But let them that love Him be as the sun when he goeth forth in his might" (Judg. 5:31). Just as the sun hasn't been extinguished, so love can't be quenched.

Chapter Fifteen

Everyone
Is Somebody's Fool

Fools are not favored in the Bible. There are over 100 references to them, and over eighty verses dealing with foolish behavior, such as: "A prating fool shall fall" (Prov. 10:10); "He that uttereth a slander is a fool" (Ibid., 10:18); "The fool shall be servant to the wise of heart" (Ibid., 11:29); "A fool layeth open his folly" (Ibid., 13:16); "A fool despiseth his father's instruction" (Ibid., 15:5); "Excellent speech becometh not a fool" (Ibid., 17:7); "He that begetteth a fool doeth it to his sorrow and the father of a fool hath no joy" (Ibid., 17:21); "Delight is not seemly for a fool" (Ibid., 19:10); "Every fool will be meddling" (Ibid., 20:3).

"Speak not in the ears of a fool: for he will despise the wisdom of thy words" (Ibid., 23:9); "As snow in summer, and as rain in harvest, so honour is not seemly for a fool" (Ibid., 26:1); "Answer not a fool according to his folly, lest thou also be like unto him" (Ibid., 26:4); "A fool uttereth all his mind" (Ibid., 29:11); "A foolish son is the heaviness of his mother" (Ibid., 10:1); "In the mouth of the foolish is a rod of pride" (Ibid., 14:3); "Go from the presence of a foolish man, when thou perceivest not in him the lips of knowledge" (Ibid., 14:7); "A foolish man despiseth his mother" (Ibid., 15:20); "If a wise man contendeth with a foolish man, whether he rage or laugh, there is no rest" (Ibid., 29:9); "He that is soon angry dealeth foolishly" (Ibid., 14:18).

"Thou hast done foolishly in lifting up thyself" (Ibid., 30:32); "The thought of foolishness is sin" (Ibid., 24:9); "A fool's wrath is presently known" (Ibid., 12:16); "A fool's lips enter into contention" (Ibid., 18:6); "A stone is heavy, and the sand weighty; but a fool's wrath is heavier than them both" (Ibid., 27:3); "A fool's voice is known by multitude of words" (Eccles. 5:3); "Shame shall be the promotion of fools" (Prov. 3:35); "Fools die for want of wisdom" (Ibid., 10:21); "It is an abomination to fools to depart from evil"; "A companion of fools shall be destroyed" (Ibid., 13:19, 20); "Fools make a mock at sin" (Ibid., 14:9); and, "The words of wise men are heart in quiet more than the cry of him that ruleth among fools" (Ibid., 9:17).

Jesus warned us, however, not to call a brother in Christ a fool, for He said, "But I say unto you, that whosoever is angry with his brother without a cause shall be in danger of the judgment: and whosoever shall say to his brother, Raca [worthless], shall be in danger of the council: but whosoever shall say, Thou fool, shall be in danger of hell fire" (Matt. 5:22).

The word "fool" in Matthew 5:22 is the Greek work *moros* (dull or stupid) from which we get our English word "moron." Paradoxically, the same Greek word is used in 1 Corinthians 3:18: "Let no man deceive himself. If any man among you seemeth to be wise in this world, let him become a fool [*moros*], that he may become wise!"

Likewise, 1 Corinthians certifies:

> God hath chosen the foolish [*moros*] things of this world
> to confound the wise; and God hath chosen the weak
> things of the world to confound the things which are
> mighty; and base things of the world, and things which
> are despised, hath God chose, yea, and things which are
> not, to bring to nought things that are: that no flesh
> should glory in His presence. (1 Cor. 3:27)

It's okay for us to be "fools for Christ" (Ibid., 4:9), "because the foolishness of God is wiser than men; and the weakness of God is stronger than men" (Ibid., 1:25). It is intriguing that in this verse the word translated "wiser" (*sophos*), when combined

with the Greek rendering of "foolishness" (*moros*) in the same
verse, gives us the English word "sophomore," a student in his
second year at high school, college, or university.

Sixteen Keys to Long Life

It's a universal desire to live as long as possible. Juan Ponce de Leon discovered Florida because the Indians had told him of an island where there existed a fountain which could restore youth to old persons. The Bible gives at least sixteen keys to long life. I put them into the acronym "WATCH FOR MUCH SEED":

1. Walk—"Ye shall walk in all the ways which the Lord your God hath commanded you, that ye may live, and that it may be well with you, and that ye may prolong your days in the land which ye shall possess" (Deut. 5:33). It's an individual walk. He's not a cookie-cutter Christ; He's not a mass-producer Messiah. "But as God hath distributed to every man, as the Lord hath called every one, so let him walk" (1 Cor. 7:17).

2. Ask—Sounds rather very elementary, but we must ask for long life. "He asked life of thee, and thou gavest it him, even length of days for ever and ever." (Ps. 21:4). "And I say unto you, Ask, and it shall be given you" (Luke 11:9).

3. Teach—"And ye shall teach them [commandments] to your children, speaking of them when thou sittest in thine house, and when thou walkest by the way, when thou liest down, and when thou risest up. And thou shalt write them upon the door posts of thine house, and upon thy gates: That your days may be multiplied,

and the days of your children, in the land which the Lord sware unto your fathers to give them as the days of heaven upon the earth" (Deut. 11:19-21).

4. Covetousness—the proscription against coveting (desiring earnestly what belongs to another) was one of the Ten Commandments: "Thou shall not covet thy neighbour's house, thou shalt not covet thy neighbour's wife, nor his manservant, nor his maidservant, nor his ox, nor his ass, nor any thing that is thy neighbour's" (Exod. 20:17). Solomon said "He that hateth covetousness shall prolong his days" (Prov. 28:16).

5. Honour mother and father—this is an important verse, as Paul said it was "the first commandment with promise (Eph. 6:2). What is the promise? "Honour thy father and thy mother: that thy days may be long upon the land which the Lord thy God giveth thee" (Exod. 20:12).

6. Fear—(i.e. reverence) is a good thing: "The fear of the Lord is the beginning of knowledge" (Prov. 1:7); "The fear of the Lord is the beginning of wisdom" (Ibid., 9:10); and, "The secret of the Lord is with them that fear Him; and He will shew them His covenant" (Ps. 25:14). But most importantly, "The fear of the Lord prolongeth days" (Prov. 10:27).

7. Obey, love, and cleave—Moses wrote "that thou mayest love the Lord thy God, and that thou mayest obey His voice, and that thou mayest cleave unto Him: for He is thy life, and the length of thy days" (Deut. 30:20).

8. Read—the Mosaic law required every king to abide by this commandment: "And it shall be, that when he sitteth upon the throne of his kingdom, that he shall write him a copy of this law in a book out of that which is before the priests and Levites: and it shall be with him, and he shall read therein all the days of his life: that he may learn to fear the Lord his God, to keep all the words of this law and these statutes, to do them:

that his heart be not lifteth up above his brethren, and that he turn not aside from the commandment, to the right hand, or to the left: to the end that he may prolong his days in the kingdom, he, and his children, in the midst of Israel" (Ibid., 17:18-20).

9. Mother (bird)—the wildest of all the keys of long life! Get this: "If a bird's nest chance to be before thee in the way in any tree, or on the ground, whether they be young ones, or eggs, and the dam [Hebrew: mother] sitting upon the young: But thou shalt in any wise let the dam [mother] go, and take the young to thee: that it may be well with thee, and that thou mayest prolong thy days" (Ibid., 22:6-7). Those who are kind to animals will live longer!

10. Understanding—"Happy is the man that findeth wisdom, and the man that getteth understanding. Length of days is in her right hand; and in her left hand riches and honour" (Prov. 3:13, 16).

11. Call—The Lord said, through David, "He shall call upon Me, and I will answer him: I will be with him in trouble, I will deliver him, and honour him. With long life will I satisfy him, and shew him My salvation" (Ps. 91:15-16).

12. Heart—Moses wrote, "Set your hearts unto all the words, which I testify among you this day, which ye shall command your children to observe and do, all the words of this law. For it is not a vain thing for you; because it is your life: and through this thing ye shall prolong your days in the land" (Deut. 30:20).

13. Statutes—"Thou shalt keep therefore His statutes and His commandments, which I command thee this day, that it may go well with thee, and with thy children after thee, and that thou mayest prolong thy days upon the earth, which the Lord thy God giveth thee, for ever" (Ibid., 4:40).

14. Equity—"But thou shalt have a perfect and just

weight, a perfect and just measure shalt thou have: that thy days may be lengthened in the land which the Lord thy God giveth thee" (Ibid., 25:15).

15. Evil tongue—"What man is he that desireth life, and loveth many days, that he may see good? Keep thy tongue from evil and thy lips from speaking guile" (Ps. 34:12-13).

16. Deceit—David wrote, "Bloody and deceitful men shall not live out half their days" (Ibid., 55:23). For the word "deceitful," most translations use either "deceitful," "treacherous," or "liars."

Chapter Seventeen

Wise to Wealth

Solomon was only a young man when he took over as king of Israel in place of his father, David. One day he and all the congregation went to Gibeon and offered a thousand burnt offerings upon the brazen altar (2 Chron. 1:3-6).

That night, God appeared to Solomon in a dream and said, "Ask what I shall give thee." Then Solomon replied,

> Thou hast shewed great mercy unto David my father, and hast made me to reign in his stead. Now, O Lord God, let Thy promise unto David my father be established: for Thou hast made me king over a people like the dust of the earth in multitude. Give me now wisdom and knowledge, that I may go out and come in before this people: for who can judge this Thy people, that is so great? (2 Chron. 1:8-10)

God then said to Solomon,

> Because this was in thine heart, and thou hast not asked riches, wealth, or honour, nor the life of your enemies,* neither yet hast asked for long life; but hast asked wisdom and knowledge for thyself, that thou mayest judge My people, over whom I have made thee king: Wisdom

---

*The only recorded battle Solomon was later engaged in, he won. Second Chronicles 8:3 states that, "Solomon went to Hamath-zobah, and prevailed against it."

and knowledge is granted unto thee; and I will give
thee riches, and wealth, and honour, such as none of
the kings have had that have been before thee, neither
shall there any after thee have the like. (Ibid., 1:11-12)

Solomon asked only for wisdom and knowledge. He received both plus riches, wealth, and honour. How rich was Solomon? First Kings 10:14 states that, "the weight of gold that came to Solomon in one year was six hundred threescore and six [666] talents of gold." Since a biblical talent was 125 pounds, that's 83,250 pounds of gold annually! Solomon reigned forty years (1 Kings 11:42). If he accumulated roughly the same amount every year, he would have collected a total of 1,670 tons of gold. That's almost one-fifth the total gold reserves of the United States!

Solomon was thus expertly qualified when he wrote: "Happy is the man that findeth wisdom, and the man that getteth understanding. Length of days is in her right hand; and in her left hand riches and honour" (Prov. 3:13, 16); "The crown of the wise is their riches" (Ibid., 14:24); and, "Through wisdom is an house builded;* and by understanding it is established: and by knowledge shall the chambers be filled with all precious and pleasant riches" (Ibid., 24:3-4). Want to be wealthy? Ask God for wisdom!

---

*Solomon spent thirteen years building his own house (1 Kings 7:1).

Chapter Eighteen

Edifying Others Brings Great Rewards

People in authority need to hear all pertinent problems so they can render effective solutions. But they also like to be told good things by their subordinates. That's why Paul wrote the church at Galatia, "Let him that is taught in the word communicate unto him that teacheth in all good things" (Gal. 6:6).

There are times when the communication should be transmitted privately. Paul wrote, "And I went up by revelation, and communicated unto them [the Jewish Christians] that gospel which I preach among the Gentiles, but privately to them which were of reputation, lest by any means I should run, or had run, in vain" (Ibid., 2:2).

Communications must always be honest, without the necessity of an oath, and should not be any longer than necessary. That's why Jesus said,

> But I say unto you, swear [take an oath] not at all; neither by heaven; for it is God's throne: nor by the earth; for it is His footstool: neither by Jerusalem; for it is the city of the great King. Neither shalt thou swear by thy head, because thou canst not make one hair white or black. But let your communication be, "Yea, yea; Nay, nay": for whatsoever is more than these cometh of evil. (Matt. 5:34-37)

Regarding the wrong types of communications, Paul said: "Be not deceived: evil communications corrupt good manners"

(1 Cor. 15:33); "Let no corrupt communication proceed out of your mouth, but that which is good to the use of edifying, that it may minister grace unto the hearers" (Eph. 4:29); and, "But now ye also put off all these; anger, wrath, malice, blasphemy, filthy communication out of your mouth" (Col. 3:8).

Communicating good things enables faith to become more effective, as per Paul: "That the communication of thy faith may become effectual by the acknowledging of every good thing which is in you in Christ Jesus" (Philem. 6).

After Jesus was resurrected, He drew near two disciples. He referred to their conversation, which was making them unhappy, by asking, "What manner of communications are these that ye have one to another, as ye walk, and are sad?" (Luke 24:17). The Lord then proceeded to open up their eyes to the Scriptures.

Yes, communication involves a sacrifice of one's self, because the communicator becomes vulnerable to how the communication will be received and responded to. It must still be done, however, because the rewards are great. Paul promised, "But to do good and to communicate forget not: for with such sacrifices God is well pleased" (Heb. 13:16). Want to make God happy? Communicate good things.

Chapter Nineteen

Don't Take It Lion Down

There are over 150 references to lions in the Bible. One day Samson was going to the town of Timnath to see a girl he fancied. Suddenly, "a young lion roared against him," at which time, "the Spirit of the Lord came mightily upon him and he rent him as he would have rent a kid, and he had nothing in his hand" (Judges 14:5-6).

Job complained to God, "Thou huntest me as a fierce lion" (Job 10:16). Later the Lord asked Job, "Wilt thou hunt the prey for the lion? Or fill the appetite of the young lions, when they couch in their dens, and abide in the covert to lie in wait?" (Ibid., 38:40). The prophet Agur listed the first of four things that go well: "a lion which is strongest among beasts, and turneth not away for any" (Prov. 30:30).

When David was trying to convince King Saul that he could take out the Philistine giant, Goliath, he said to Saul, "Thy servant kept his father's sheep, and there came a lion and a bear, and took a lamb out of the flock: and I went out after him, and smote him, and delivered it out of his mouth: and when he arose against me, I caught him by his beard, and smote him, and slew him" (1 Sam. 17:34-35).

After King Saul and his son, Jonathan, were tragically killed on the battlefield, David eulogized, "Saul and Jonathan were lovely and pleasant in their lives, and in their death they were not divided: they were swifter than eagles, they were stronger than lions" (2 Sam. 1:23). Later, one of David's soldiers, Benaiah, "slew two lion-like men of Moab," and on another occasion, "went down also and slew a lion in the midst of a pit in time of snow" (2 Sam. 23:20).

It's no wonder David included lions among the subjects of his writings: "The young lions do lack, and suffer hunger: but they that seek the Lord shall not want any good thing" (Ps. 34:10); "With hypocritical mockers in feasts, they gnashed upon me with their teeth. Lord, how long wilt Thou look on? Rescue my soul from their destruction, my darling from the lions" (Ibid., 35:16-17); and, "For He shall give His angels charge over Thee, to keep Thee in all thy ways. They shall bear thee up in their hands, lest Thou dash thy foot against a stone. Thou shalt tread upon the lion and adder" (Ibid., 91:11-13).

The king of Assyria brought men from Babylon and other heathen kingdoms. He placed them, instead of the children of Israel, in the cities of Samaria. But it came to pass, "at the beginning of their dwelling there, that they feared not the Lord: therefore the Lord sent lions among them and slew some of them" (2 Kings 17:25).

In his palace decor, King Solomon, "made a great throne of ivory, and overlaid it with the best gold. And twelve lions stood there on one side and on the other upon the six steps: there was not the like made in any kingdom" (1 Kings 10:20). Solomon, like his father, wrote much about lions:

"As a roaring lion, and a ranging bear; so is a wicked ruler over the poor people" (Prov. 28:15); "For to him that is joined to all the living there is hope: for a living dog is better than a dead lion" (Eccles. 9:4); and, "Come with me from Lebanon, my spouse, with me from Lebanon: look from the top of Amana, from the top of Shenir and Hermon, from the lions' dens, from the mountains of the leopards" (Song of Solomon 4:8).

Isaiah wrote: "Like as the lion and the young lion roaring on his prey, when a multitude of shepherds is called forth against him, he will not be afraid of their voice, nor abase himself for the noise of them: so shall the Lord of hosts come down to fight for mount Zion, and for the hill thereof" (Isa. 31:4); and,

An highway shall be there, and a way, and it shall be
called, "The way of holiness"; the unclean shall not pass
over it; but it shall be for those: the wayfaring men,
though fools, shall not err therein. No lion shall be
there, nor any ravenous beast shall go up thereon, it
shall not be found there; but the redeemed shall walk
there. (Ibid., 35:8-9)

The little-known Amos asked: "Will a lion roar in the
forest, when he hath no prey? Will a young lion cry out of his
den, if he have taken nothing?" (Amos 3:4); and, "The lion
hath roared, who will not fear? The Lord God hath spoken,
who can but prophesy?" (Ibid., 3:8).

Another minor minister, Micah, mentioned, "And the remnant of Jacob shall be among the Gentiles in the midst of many
people as a lion among the beasts of the forest, as a young lion
among the flocks of sheep: who, if he go through, both treadeth
down, and teareth in pieces, and none can deliver" (Micah 5:8).

Paul penned, "by me the preaching might be fully known,
and that all the Gentiles might hear: and I was delivered out of
the mouth of the lion. And the Lord shall deliver me from
every evil work, and will preserve me unto His heavenly kingdom" (2 Tim. 4:17-18).

David wrote,

Though an host should encamp against me, my heart
shall not fear: though war should rise against me, in
this will I be confident. One thing have I desired of the
Lord, that will I seek after; that I may dwell in the
house of the Lord all the days of my life, to behold the
beauty of the Lord, and to inquire in His temple. (Ps.
27:3-4)

The word translated "confident" in this verse is the same
word rendered "bold" in: "The wicked flee when no man
pursueth: but the righteous are bold as a lion" (Prov. 28:1).

Chapter Twenty

Dead Flies Stink

There are ten references to flies in the Bible. All but one refer to the event when swarms of flies were sent against the Egyptians during the time of Moses.* The Hebrew word used in those instances is *arob*. While most Bible translations render *arob* simply as "flies," others use: "gnats," "gadflies" (a large fly that bites livestock), "horseflies," "insects," or "beetles." Interestingly, *Strong's Concordance* interprets *arob* as "mosquito."

One of the names for Satan is *baal-zebuwb* (Old Testament) and beelzebub (New Testament), and they both mean, "lord of the *flies*." The only reference to flies in the Bible that doesn't refer to the particular plague in Egypt is found in Ecclesiastes: "Dead flies cause the ointment of the apothecary to send forth a stinking savour: so doth a little folly him that is in reputation for wisdom and honour" (Eccles. 10:1). The word "flies" used here is not *arob*, but *zebuwb*, the same Hebrew word used in *baal-zebuwb*, above. *Zebuwb* refers to the common housefly.

A person's reputation is a very important thing. Solomon supplied: "A good name is rather to be chosen than great riches, and loving favour rather than silver and gold" (Prov. 22:1); and, "a good name is better than precious ointment" (Eccles. 7:10).

---

*See Exodus 8:21-31.

Luke let us know that: "Gamaliel, a doctor of the law, had in reputation among all the people" (Acts 5:34); the twelve apostles called disciples to them and said, "It is not reason that we should leave the word of God, and serve tables. Wherefore, brethren, look ye out among you seven men of honest report, full of the Holy Ghost and wisdom, whom we may appoint over this business" (Ibid., 6:2-3); "Cornelius the centurion, a just man, and one that feareth God, and of good report among all the nation of the Jews, was warned from God by an holy angel" (Ibid., 10:22).

Paul wrote: "And one Ananias, a devout man according to the law, having a good report of all the Jews which dwelt there, came unto me, and stood, and said unto me, 'Brother Saul, receive thy sight.' And the same hour I looked upon him" (Ibid., 22:12-3); "I went up by revelation, communicated unto them that gospel which I preach among the Gentiles, but privately to them which of reputation, lest by any means I should run, or had run, in vain" (Gal. 2:2); "This is a true saying, 'If a man desire the office a bishop, he desireth a good work. Moreover he must have a good report of them which are without'" (1 Tim. 3:1, 7); and, "Demetrius hath good report of all men, and of the truth itself" (3 John 12).

The greater your position in society, the more others will scrutinize you and hold you accountable. Because of that, your stink will be greater if you make a mistake! Christ confirmed this when He said, "for unto whomever much is given, of him shall be much required: and to whom men have committed much, of him they will ask the more" (Luke 12:48).

Chapter Twenty-One

The Net

A net, an openwork fabric used to trap birds, fish, etc., is mentioned forty-nine times in the Bible, mostly in negative contexts. Job, vexed by his friends who reproached him ten times, said, "Know now that God hath overthrown me, and hath compassed me about with His net. Behold, I cry out of wrong, but I am not heard: I cry aloud, but there is no judgment" (Job 19:6-7).

David's writings list ten references to nets, including: "Mine eyes are ever toward the Lord; for He shall pluck my feet out of the net" (Ps. 25:15); "Pull me out of the net that they have laid privily for me: for Thou art my strength" (Ibid., 31:4); "For without cause have they hid for me their net in a pit, which without cause they have digged for my soul. Let destruction come upon him at unawares; and let his net that he hid catch himself" (Ibid., 35:7-8); and, "Let the wicked fall into their own nets, whilst that I withal escape" (Ibid., 141:10).

Solomon said sagaciously: "Indeed, it is useless to spread the net in the eyes of any bird" (Prov. 1:17, NAS); "The wicked desireth the net of evil men: but the root of the righteous yieldeth fruit" (Ibid., 12:12); "A man that flattereth his neighbour spreadeth a net for his feet" (Ibid., 29:5); and, "I find more bitter than death the woman, whose heart is snares and nets, and her hands as bands: whoso pleaseth God shall escape from her; but the sinner shall be taken by her" (Eccles. 7:26).

Most of the references to nets are found in the New Testament. Matthew 4:18-19 states, "Jesus, walking by the sea of Galilee, saw two brethren, Simon called Peter, and Andrew his brother, casting a net into the sea: for they were fishers. And He saith unto them, 'Follow Me, and I will make you fishers of men.'"

Two verses later, Matthew wrote, "And going on from thence, He saw the other two brethren, James the son of Zebedee, and John his brother, in a ship with Zebedee their father, mending their nets; and He called them." These references to men "casting" and "mending" nets reveal that the Lord chose industrious people to work for Him. Jesus also said, "The kingdom of heaven is like unto a net, that was cast into the sea, and gathered of every kind: which, when it was full, they drew to shore, and sat down, and gathered the good into vessels" (Matt. 13:47-48).

There are two similar fish stories in the New Testament that bring home something important. The first is mentioned in Luke, chapter five. Christ was being pushed against a lake by a huge following of people. Seeing two empty ships, Jesus entered into one and taught the multitude from its deck. After Christ was through speaking, He said to Simon, one of the fishermen, "Launch out into the deep, and let down your nets" (Luke 5:4). Simon replied, "Master, we have toiled all the night, and have taken nothing: nevertheless at Thy word I will let down the net" (Luke 5:5). The fishermen then caught such a "great multitude" of fish that their net broke and the ship was so full it began to sink. Simon Peter, James, and John were so astonished at the amount of fish that were miraculously taken up that they left their jobs and followed Jesus (Luke 5:9-11).

The second fishing incident happened after Jesus was resurrected. He again showed up on a morning again after some fishermen had labored all night and caught nothing. This time, they didn't recognize Jesus at first. He asked, "Children, have ye any meat?" They answered Him, "No." Jesus then said, "Cast the net on the right side of the ship, and ye shall find." They threw in the net and then weren't able to draw it in for the huge haul. The Bible records that there were 153 great fish caught. This time the net did not break. It was at that moment Peter recognized him as the Lord (John 21:5-6).

Solomon wrote, "For man knoweth not his time: as the fishes that are taken in an evil net, and as the birds that are caught in the snare; so are the sons of men snared in an evil time, when it falleth suddenly upon them" (Eccles. 9:12). However, as Jesus caused the fishermen's nets to increase their normal catches because they followed His instructions, so He is also able to lengthen our allotted lifespans if we do what He suggests!

Chapter Twenty-Two

Supporting Roles

After Joseph's jealous brothers sold him to some Ishmaelite merchants, he came into the possession of Potiphar, an officer of the Pharaoh. When his master saw that the Lord prospered everything that Joseph did, he made him overseer of all his holdings (Gen. 39:1-5).

When Potiphar's wife falsely accused Joseph of sexual harassment, he was cast into Pharaoh's prison. Again, because the Lord was with Joseph, he ended up in charge of all the prisoners (Gen. 39:22). Later, he did a service for one of Pharaoh's chief employees (Ibid., 40:9-13), and, two years later, for the Pharaoh himself (Ibid., 41:16, 24). After thirteen years* of service to others, Joseph finally became a ruler himself (Ibid., 41:43).

Joshua was a minister to Moses for many years (Exod. 24:13), but eventually he took Moses' place and, before Moses died, he gave Joshua this charge: "Be strong and of a good courage: for thou shalt bring the children of Israel into the land which I sware unto them" (Deut. 31:23).

Samuel, as a child, "did minister unto the Lord before Eli the priest" (1 Sam. 2:11). When he became a young man, "all Israel from Dan even to Beersheba knew that Samuel was established to be a prophet of the Lord" (Ibid., 3:20).

---

*Compare Genesis 37:2 with 41:46.

For several years Elisha, "poured water on the hands of Elijah" (2 Kings 3:11) and assisted him in various other ways. It came to pass, "when the LORD would take up Elijah into heaven by a whirlwind" (Ibid., 2:1), that Elisha said to his master, "I pray thee, let a double portion of thy spirit be upon me" (Ibid., 2:9). Elisha ended up performing twice the number of miracles as his former teacher.

David served king Saul as an "armourbearer" (1 Sam. 16:21). David also did service as a musician. The Bible states that whenever, "the evil spirit from God was upon Saul, that David took an harp, and played with his hand: so Saul was refreshed, and was well, and the evil spirit departed from him" (1 Sam. 16:23). Eventually, David was crowned king in Saul's place.

To the elders of the church at Ephesus, Paul declared, "I have shewed you all things, how that so labouring ye ought to support the weak" (Acts 20:35). And to the church of the Thessalonians he wrote, "Now we exhort you, brethren, warn them that are unruly, comfort the feebleminded, support the weak" (1 Thess. 5:14).

The Greek word for "support," used in the two verses immediately above, is the same (or similar) Greek word that is translated "hold" in: "No man can serve two masters: for either he will hate the one, and despise the other; or else he will hold to the one, and despise the other. Ye cannot serve God and mammon" (Matt. 6:24); "holding" in, "Holding fast the faithful word as he hath been taught, that he may be able by sound doctrine both to exhort and to convince the gainsayers" (Titus 1:9); and "helps" in, "Now ye are the body of Christ, and members in particular. And God hath set some in the church, first apostles, secondarily prophets, thirdly teachers, after that miracles, then gifts of healing, helps, governments, diversities of tongues" (1 Cor. 12:27-28).

When the heavenly academy hands out its awards someday, those who were only cast in supporting roles on earth will receive their much-deserved recognition.

Chapter Twenty-Three

Don't Throw
Pearls Before Pigs

In Old Testament times, God's law prohibited the eating of pigs. Moses mandated, "And the swine, because it divideth the hoof, yet cheweth not the cud, it is unclean unto you: ye shall not eat of their flesh, nor touch their dead carcase" (Deut. 14:8).* And, making a metaphor regarding tact and refinement, Solomon said, "As a jewel of gold in a swine's snout, so is a fair woman which is without discretion" (Prov. 11:22).

There are twenty references to swine in the Bible and ten to pearls. Job wrote,

> But where shall wisdom be found? And where is the place of understanding? Man knoweth not the price thereof; neither is it found in the land of the living. The depth saith, "It is not in me": and the sea saith, "It is not in me." It cannot be gotten for gold, neither shall silver be weighed for the price thereof. It cannot be valued with the gold of Ophir, with the precious onyx, or the sapphire. The gold and the crystal cannot equal it: and the exchange of it shall not be for jewels or fine gold.

---

*The New Testament changed such food proscriptions. Paul wrote, "Every creature of God is good, and nothing to be refused, if it be received with thanksgiving" (1 Tim. 4:4).

received with thanksgiving" (1 Tim. 4:4).

> No mention shall be made of coral, or of pearls: for the
> price of wisdom is above rubies. The topaz of Ethiopia
> shall not equal it, neither shall it be valued with pure
> gold. (Job 28:12-19)

Jesus said, "The kingdom of heaven is like unto a merchant
man, seeking goodly pearls: who, when he had found one pearl
of great price, went and sold all that he had, and bought it"
(Matt. 13:45-46).

Paul wrote, "That women adorn themselves in modest ap-
parel, with shamefacedness and sobriety; not with broided hair,
or gold, or pearls, or costly array; but (which becometh women
professing godliness) with good works" (1 Tim. 2:9-10).

Referring to the twelve entrances to the holy city, New
Jerusalem, John said, "And the twelve gates were twelve pearls:
every several gate was of one pearl: and the street of the city
was pure* gold, as it were transparent glass" (Rev. 21:21).

Jesus told a story of two sons. The younger one asked his
father for his inheritance and then left home. He later wasted
his substance with riotous living. After he had spent all he had,
a famine broke out where he was residing and he began to be
hungry. The younger son then went and, "joined himself to a
citizen of that country; and he sent him into his fields to feed
swine" (Luke 15:15). For a Jewish boy to feed pigs was the
utmost disgrace. It was then that the younger son decided to go
back home and ask for his father's forgiveness.

Swine don't know the value of pearls or other precious
stones. To them they are like pebbles—they can't be eaten so
what good are they? That's why Jesus said, "Give not that
which is holy unto the dogs, neither cast ye your pearls before
swine, lest they trample them under their feet, and turn again
and rend you" (Matt. 7:6).

You must be careful who you divulge your deep-seated
desires to; who you share your sensitive secrets with; who you
broadcast your beloved beliefs to—lest the things particularly
precious to you be rudely rejected.

---

*The Greek word used here doesn't mean unalloyed, but "clean."

Chapter Twenty-Four

Reward Offered

There are almost 100 references to rewards in the Bible. In a vision, the Lord told Abraham, "I am thy shield, and thy exceeding great reward" (Gen. 15:1). The Hebrew word used here for "reward" means "*payment* of a contract." The Lord later honored that "contract" and made Abraham a "father of many nations" (Ibid., 17:4).

David described, "The statutes of the Lord are right, rejoicing the heart . . . and in keeping of them is great reward" (Ps. 19:8, 11). While Solomon declared: "To him that soweth righteousness is a sure reward" (Prov. 11:18); "My son, eat thou honey, because it is good; and the honeycomb, which is sweet to thy taste: so shall the knowledge of wisdom be unto thy soul: when thou hast found it, then there shall be a reward, and thy expectation shall not be cut off" (Ibid., 24:13-14); and, "If thine enemy be hungry, give him bread to eat; and if he be thirsty, give him water to drink: for thou shalt heap coals of fire upon his head, and the Lord shall reward thee" (Ibid., 25:21-22).

Christ said: "But when thou doest alms, let not thy left hand know what thy right hand doeth: that thine alms may be in secret: and thy Father which seeth in secret Himself shall reward thee openly" (Matt. 6:3-4);

> He that receiveth a prophet in the name of a prophet shall receive a prophet's reward; and he that receiveth a righteous man in the name of a righteous man shall receive a righteous man's reward. And whosoever shall

give a drink unto one of these little ones a cup of cold water only in the name of a disciple, verily I say unto you, he shall in no wise lose his reward. (Ibid., 10:41-42)

Blessed are ye, when men shall hate you, and when they shall separate you from their company, and shall reproach you, and cast out your name as evil, for the Son of man's sake. Rejoice ye in that day, and leap for joy: for, behold, your reward is great in heaven: for in like manner did their fathers unto the prophets. (Luke 6:22-23)

Paul proclaimed: "Every man shall receive his own reward according to his own labour" (1 Cor. 3:8); and, "Cast not away therefore your confidence, which hath great recompense of reward" (Heb. 10:35). But Paul really hit home with: "He that cometh to God must believe that He is, and that He is a rewarder of them that diligently seek Him" (Ibid., 11:6). The Lord wants us to come to Him expecting remuneration—as long as we are willing to work for it.

Chapter Twenty-Five

Money Answers All Things

There are over 120 references of money in the Bible. When Abraham's wife Sarah died, he told the people of Hebron that he wanted to buy a cave in which to bury his wife. He told them he would give, "as much money as it is worth" (Gen. 23:9).

During the seven years of famine in the land of Egypt, Joseph sold the corn which had been stored up. He then, "gathered up all the money that was found in the land of Egypt, and in the land of Canaan, for the corn which they bought" (Ibid., 47:14). Joseph then, "brought the money into Pharaoh's house" (Ibid.).

A Mosaic commandment (and a forerunner to our modern laws regarding negligence and damages) stated that, "If a man shall open a pit, or if a man shall dig a pit, and not cover it and an ox or an ass fall therein; the owner of the pit shall make it good, and give money unto the owner of them; and the dead beast shall be his" (Exodus 21:33).

Predating our modern laws regarding bailment, Jewish law held that,

> If a man [bailor] shall deliver unto his neighbour [bailee] money or stuff to keep, and it be stolen out of the man's house; if the thief be found, let him pay double. If the thief be not found, then the master of the house

shall be brought unto the judges, to see whether he have put his hand unto his neighbour's good. (Ibid., 22:7-8)

After Job's trial was concluded, and the Lord had given Job twice as many possessions as he had originally owned, the Scripture states that, "Then came there unto him all his brethren, and all his sisters, and all they that had been of his acquaintance before, and did eat bread with him in his house: and . . . every man also gave him a piece of money, and every one an earring of gold" (Job 42:11).

Solomon wrote, "For wisdom is a defense, and money is a defense: but the excellency of knowledge is that wisdom giveth life to them that have it" (Eccles. 7:12).

In the book of Isaiah, the Lord implored,

Ho, every one that thirsteth, come ye to the waters, and he that hath no money; come ye, buy, and eat; yea, come, buy wine and milk without money and without price. Wherefore do ye spend money for that which is not bread? And your labour for that which satisfieth not? Hearken diligently unto Me, and eat ye that which is good, and let your soul delight itself in fatness. (Isa. 55:1-2)

Jesus told a parable about a certain nobleman who was angry with the man who had hidden the money he had given to him. The nobleman said to the man, "Wherefore then gavest not my money into the bank, that at my coming I might have required my own with usury?" (Luke 19:23).

Even though the Bible states that "the love* of money is the root of all evil" (1 Tim. 6:10), Solomon put things into perspective when he said, "A feast is made for laughter, and wine maketh merry: but money answereth all things" (Eccles. 10:19).

---

*Notice that it doesn't say that "*money* is the root of all evil," as is often misquoted, but that "the *love* of money is the root of all evil."

Chapter Twenty-Six

The Path to Promotion

Promotion is always a favorite subject of conversation in the workplace. Shadrach, Meshach, and Abednego already had positions of authority in the province of Babylon. However, they refused to obey an order from their superior because of their religious convictions. After God delivered them from a fiery trial, the Bible says that, "the king promoted Shadrach, Meshach, and Abednego, in the province of Babylon" (Dan. 3:30). The Hebrew word used for "promotion" in this verse is the same word that is translated "prosper" in these two Scriptures:

"And the keeper of the prison committed to Joseph's hand all the prisoners that were in the prison; and whatsoever they did there, he was the doer of it. The keeper of the prison looked not to any thing that was under his hand; because the Lord was with him, and that which he did, the Lord made it to prosper" (Gen. 39:22-23); and,

"Then Solomon sat on the throne of the Lord as king instead of David his father, and prospered; and all Israel obeyed him. And all the princes, and the mighty men, and all the sons likewise of king David, submitted themselves unto Solomon the king" (1 Chron. 29:23-24). Clearly, Joseph and Solomon were elevated in their employment.

Solomon sustained, "shame shall be the promotion of fools." The Hebrew word for "shame" here is the same word that is translated:

As "dishonour" in: "But whoso committeth adultery with a woman lacketh understanding: he that doeth it destroyeth his own soul. A wound and dishonour shall he get; and his reproach shall not be wiped away" (Prov. 6:32-33);

As "ignominy" in: "when the wicked cometh, then cometh also contempt, and with ignominy reproach" (Ibid., 18:3); and,

As "reproach" in: "Cast out the scorner, and contention shall go out; yea, strife and reproach shall cease" (Ibid., 22:10). That is to say, "adulterers," "ignominious" persons, and "scorners" will be promoted—with shame.

Solomon also said, "Wisdom is the principal thing; therefore get wisdom: Exalt her, and she shall promote thee: she shall bring thee to honour, when thou dost embrace her" (Ibid., 4:7, 8). The word "embrace" here is the same Hebrew word used for "embrace" in, "Why wilt thou, my son, be ravished with a strange woman, and embrace the bosom of a stranger?" (Ibid., 5:20).

I believe Solomon's dad, David, had the decisive word on the matter: "Lift not up your horn on high: speak not with a stiff neck. For promotion cometh neither from the west, nor from the east, nor from the south. But God is judge: He putteth down one, and setteth up another" (Ps. 75:5-7).

Chapter Twenty-Seven

A Good God

For those readers who experienced bad childhood relationships with their earthly fathers (or fathers-in-law), it's hard to imagine a heavenly Father as offering anything better. But I'm here to tell you, God is good!

Though the biblical Joseph was sold into slavery by his jealous brothers, then falsely accused by his master's wife and cast into prison, he still understood that God was good. That's why he told his brothers, "Ye thought evil against me; but God meant it unto good, to bring to pass, as it is this day, to save much people alive" (Gen. 50:20).

Moses, who knew much about God's goodness, maintained: "The Lord commanded us to do all these statutes, to fear the Lord our God, for our good always, that He might preserve us alive" (Deut. 6:24);

"Who fed thee in the wilderness with manna, which thy fathers knew not, that He might humble thee, and that He might prove thee, to do thee good at thy latter end" (Ibid., 8:16); and,

"For the Lord will again rejoice over thee for good, as He rejoiced over thy fathers" (Ibid., 30:9). In like manner, Moses' successor, Joshua, wrote, "There failed not ought of any good thing which the Lord had spoken unto the house of Israel; all came to pass" (Josh. 21:45).

Of all authors in the Bible, no one mentioned more about the goodness of the Lord than, you guessed it, David. He wrote:

"Surely goodness and mercy shall follow me all the days of my life" (Ps. 23:6). "Good and upright is the Lord: therefore will He teach sinners in the way" (Ibid., 25:8). "I had fainted, unless I had believed to see the goodness of the Lord in the land of the living" (Ibid., 27:13).

"Oh how great is Thy goodness, which Thou hast laid up for them that fear Thee; which Thou hast wrought for them that trust in Thee before the sons of men!" (Ibid., 31:19). "The earth is full of the goodness of the Lord" (Ibid., 33:5). "They that seek the Lord shall not want any good thing" (Ibid., 34:10).

"Why boasteth thou thyself in mischief, O mighty man? The goodness of God endureth continually" (Ibid., 52:1). "Thou crownest the year with Thy goodness" (Ibid., 65:11). "Thou, O God, hast prepared of Thy goodness for the poor" (Ibid., 68:10). "Hear me, O Lord; for Thy lovingkindness is good" (Ibid., 69:16).

"No good thing will He withhold from them that walk uprightly" (Ibid., 84:11). "He satisfieth the longing soul, and filleth the hungry soul with goodness" (Ibid., 107:9); and, "The Lord is good to all: and His tender mercies are over all His works" (Ibid., 145:9).

The Lord told Jeremiah: "I will satiate the soul of the priests with fatness, and My people shall be satisfied with My goodness" (Jer. 31:14); and, "I will give them one heart, and one way, that they may fear Me for ever, for the good of them, and of their children after them" (Ibid., 32:39).

My two favorite Scriptures dealing with the goodness of the Lord were written by Paul: "We know that all things work together for good to them that love God, to them who are the called according to His purpose" (Rom. 8:28); and, "Whatsoever good thing any man doeth, the same shall he receive of the Lord" (Eph. 6:8).

Chapter Twenty-Eight

Merry Medicine

The first mention of mirth in the Bible was in the thirty-first chapter of Genesis. God told Jacob that He had seen how his father-in-law, Laban, had mistreated him and He wanted Jacob to go back to the land of his father in Canaan. Jacob left and carried away all the cattle and goods which he had acquired. He had been gone three days when Laban found out he had fled. Laban overtook Jacob and said, "Wherefore didst thou flee away secretly, and steal way from me; and didst not tell me, that I might have sent thee away with mirth, and with songs, with tabret, and with harp?" (Gen. 31:27).

After Solomon dedicated the house of God, "he sent the people away into their tents, glad and merry in heart for the goodness that the Lord had shewed unto David, and to Solomon, and to Israel His people" (2 Chron. 7:10).

After Ezra and Nehemiah read the book of the law of Moses to the people, then "all the people went their way to eat, and to drink, and to send portions, and to make great mirth, because they had understood the words that were declared unto them" (Neh. 8:12).

Solomon wrote: "I commended mirth, because a man hath no better thing under the sun, than to eat, and to drink, and to be merry: for that shall abide with him of his labour the days of his life, which God giveth him under the sun" (Eccles. 8:15); "A merry heart maketh a cheerful countenance" (Prov. 15:13); "He that is of a merry heart hath a continual feast" (Ibid.,

15:15); and, "A merry heart doeth good like a medicine" (Ibid., 17:22).

When the Pharisees and scribes put down Jesus because He was associating with publicans and sinners, Jesus told the parable of the prodigal son. A man had two sons. The younger one asked for his inheritance, and then went to a far country where he, "wasted his substance with riotous living" (Luke 15:13). After he had spent all that he had, a famine arose in the land. He found himself feeding pigs and became famished.

Realizing that his father's servants were better off than he, the prodigal son decided to return home, confess to his father that he had sinned against him and heaven, and ask to be made one of the hired workers. While he was yet a great way off, the father had compassion on him and ran to meet him. The father then said to the servants, "Bring hither the fatted calf, and kill it; and let us eat, and be merry: for this my son was dead, and is alive again; he was lost, and is found. And they began to be merry" (Luke 15:23-4).

Christ then went on to explain the allegory (the same meaning of the parables of the lost sheep and lost coin): "Joy shall be in heaven over one sinner that repenteth" (Ibid., 15:7). In other words, the Lord is made merry when His children return to Him!

Chapter Twenty-Nine

The Power of One

One man, Noah, "found grace in the eyes of the Lord" (Gen. 6:8), and saved the human race from extinction.

One man, Abraham, left his own country to go to a land that he had never been to before, and there he became the father of a great nation (Ibid., 12:1-2).

One man, Joseph, became a ruler in the most powerful nation in the world (Ibid., 41:42-43).

One man, Moses, was called by God to lead over two million people out of the land of Egypt. (Aaron later joined his brother only after Moses kept making excuses for not wanting to do the job; see Exod. 4:10-14.)

One man, David, single-handedly killed a giant of a soldier and later became king of an entire country (1 Sam. 17:49; 2 Sam. 5:3).

One woman, Mary, had an angel appear and tell her that she would bring forth a child, the Son of the Highest, Who would reign over the house of Jacob forever (Luke 1:31-33).

The Bible lists scores of other obscure individuals who performed great tasks. Indeed, God seems to especially enjoy that method of operation. Below is a list of companies, founded predominately by individuals, with names that have become household words:

Dwight Baldwin (pianos)	Adolf Bayer (aspirin)	Alexander Graham Bell (telephone)
William Edward Boeing (airplanes)	Henry Brooks (clothier)	John M. Brunswick (billiard tables)
David Dunbar Buick (automobiles)	Joseph Campbell (soups)	Dr. Willis Carrier (air conditioners)
Louis Chevrolet (car designer)	Walter Chrysler (automobiles)	William Colgate (soap/toothpaste)
Rudolf Diesel (diesel engine)	Sanford Dole (pineapple company)	Herbert Henry Dow (chemical company)
John Boyd Dunlop (tires)	Ole Evinrude (outboard motors)	Leo Fender (guitars)
Debbie Fields (cookies)	Harvey S. Firestone (tire and rubber company)	James Folger (coffee)
Henry Ford (cars)	Dan Gerber (baby food)	King Camp Gillette (razors)
Benjamin Franklin Goodrich (tires)	Charles Goodyear (tires)	Rev. Sylvester Graham (graham crackers)
Henry John Heinz (catsup and sundries)	Milton Hershey (chocolate)	John Hertz (rent-a-car company)
John Van Heusen (shirts)	W. H. Hoover (vacuums)	Candido Jacuzzi (whirlpool bath)
Carl Jantzen (swimwear)	S. C. Johnson (wax)	Will Keith Kellogg (cereals)
James Lewis Kraft (food products)	Herman W. Lay (potato chips)	Bill Lear (jets)

Joshua Lionel (train sets)	Thomas Lipton (tea)	Edward Lloyd (London insurance co.)
Joseph M. Long (drug stores)	Rowland H. Macy (department store)	Fred Maytag (washing machines)
George Merck (chemical company)	J. Sterling Morton (salt)	Eli Olds (automobiles)
Elisha Otis (elevators)	George Safford Parker (pens)	James C. Penny (department store)
Charles Pillsbury (food products)	Ferdinand Porsche (automobiles)	C. W. Post (cereals)
Sol Price (wholesale store)	Richard Reynolds (aluminum)	Adolphe Sax (saxophone)
Jacob Schick (first electric razor)	Mary See (candy)	Johnson Shakey (pizza)
Zalmon Simmons (mattress)	Jerome Smucker (jams and jellies)	Heinrich Steinway (pianos)
Charles Tiffany (jewelry)	Earl Tupper (Tupperware)	William Voit (athletic rubber balls)
Charles Walgreen (drug stores)	A. Montgomery Ward (department store)	Dr. Thomas Welch (grape juice)
Stephen Whitman (chocolate samplers)	F. W. Woolworth (5 & 10 stores)	William Wrigley (gum)

Chapter Thirty

How to Open Heaven's Windows of Blessing

The first mention of paying tithes* on any increase (e.g., wages, gifts of money, etc.) was in Genesis 14. There it tells how Melchizedek, a priest and king of Salem, brought bread and wine to Abraham as he returned from rescuing his nephew, Lot. Melchizedek said to Abraham, "Blessed be the most high God, which hath delivered thine enemies into thy hand" (Gen. 14:19). In the same verse it says that Abraham, "gave him tithes of all."

The Lord later formalized the commandment of paying tithes when He told Moses, "And all the tithe of the land, whether of the seed of the land, or of the fruit of the tree, is the Lord's: it is holy unto the Lord. And concerning the tithe of the herd, or of the flock, even of whatsoever passeth under the rod, the tenth shall be holy unto the Lord" (Lev. 27:30, 32).

Moses told the people,

> But when ye go over Jordan, and dwell in the land which the Lord your God giveth you to inherit, and when He giveth you rest from all your enemies round about, so that ye dwell in safety; then there shall be a place which the Lord your God shall choose to cause His name to dwell there; thither shall ye bring all that

---

*Hebrew: *tenth*.

I command you; your burnt offerings, and your sacrifices, your tithes, and the heave offering of your hand.
(Deut. 12:10-11)

Christ chastised the religious leaders, even though they
were paying their tithes. He said, "Woe unto you, scribes and
Pharisees, hypocrites! For ye pay tithe of mint and anise and
cumin, and have omitted the weightier matters of the law,
judgment, mercy, and faith: these ought ye have done, and not
to leave the other [tithing] undone" (Matt. 23:23).

Tithing must also be done with the proper attitude. Christ
told a parable in which a Pharisee prayed "with himself" (Luke
18:11). The religious leader thanked God that he was not as
other evil men, saying, "I fast twice in the week, I give tithes
of all that I possess" (Ibid., 18:12). Jesus said that the publican,
who was standing afar off from the Pharisee, was more justified
than the Pharisee because he humbled himself and said, "God
be merciful to me a sinner" (Ibid., 18:13).

Malachi, who wrote the last book in the Old Testament,
mentioned one of the most astounding promises regarding financial rewards in the entire Bible: "Bring ye all the tithes into
the storehouse, that there may be meat in Mine house, and
prove Me now herewith, saith the Lord of hosts, if I will not
open you the windows of heaven, and pour you out a blessing,
that there shall not be room enough to receive it" (Mal. 3:10).

The way I see it, God loves His ministers of the gospel and
wants them to prosper. In order to do so, God will endow
Christians so we can bless them. The more we make, the more
they make! Example: if you earn $100,000 a year, the church
gets $10,000. Result: you keep $90,000.* But if you acquire
$1,000,000 annually, the church then receives $100,000 (what
you used to make) and you keep $900,000! Look at it this way:
if you pay tithes, it's in God's interest to increase your income!

---

*That's before the government takes its chunk.

Chapter Thirty-One

A Friend to Fasting

Great men in the Bible did it; Samuel fasted (1 Sam. 7:5-6), David missed meals (2 Sam. 12:16), as did Jehoshaphat (2 Chron. 20:3), Ezra (Ezra 8:21), and Nehemiah (Neh. 9:1).

The Lord encouraged fasting, for He said, "Turn ye even to Me with all your heart, and with fasting, and with weeping, and with mourning: and rend your heart, and not your garments, and turn unto the Lord your God: for He is gracious and merciful, slow to anger, and of great kindness and repenteth Him of the evil" (Joel 2:12-13).

People fasted various lengths of time. Esther fasted three days (Esther 4:16); valiant men of Jabeshgilead fasted seven days after Saul was killed (1 Sam. 31:13); Daniel fasted twenty-one days (Dan. 10:2-3); and Moses fasted *eighty* days—*two* successive forty day fasts! (Exod. 34:28 and Deut. 9:18).

Most fasts, however, were only one day. Jeremiah seemed to refer to a regularly scheduled fasting day, when he told the king to read the words of the Lord, "upon the fasting day" (Jer. 36:6).

Many medical doctors* maintain that there are many health benefits to be gained from fasting under controlled conditions. In addition, regarding the salutary results to the soul,

---

*E.g. Dr. Herbert M. Shelton ("Fasting Can Save Your Life").

David discerned: "I humbled my soul with fasting" (Ps. 35:13); and, "I wept, and chastened my soul with fasting" (Ibid., 69:10).

In the New Testament, Cornelius, a Gentile, was fasting when suddenly, an angel appeared to him and said, "Cornelius, thy prayer is heard, and thine alms are had in remembrance in the sight of God" (Ibid., 10:30-31). Paul and Barnabas fasted before they ordained elders in the churches they visited (Ibid., 14:23). Paul, who had a powerful ministry, said that he underwent "fasting often" (2 Cor. 11:27). Earlier in the same book, he wrote, "In all things approving ourselves as the ministers of God, in much patience, in afflictions, in necessities, in distresses, . . . in watchings, in fastings" (Ibid., 6:4-5).

There is only one recorded incident of Jesus fasting (though He must have fasted often). It was just before He started His ministry, and it was forty days in length. When His disciples, who had already performed many miracles, could not cast out a lunatic spirit in a particular child, they brought him to Jesus. After the Master cast out the spirit the disciples asked Him, "Why could not we cast him out?" (Matt. 17:14-20). Jesus said, "Because of your unbelief." He then went on to say, "Howbeit this kind goeth not out but by prayer and fasting" (Ibid, 17:21).

Disciples of both John and the Pharisees, who were used to fasting, once came to Jesus and asked, "Why do the disciples of John and of the Pharisees fast, but Thy disciples fast not?" (Mark 2:18). Jesus answered, "Can the children of the Bridegroom fast, while the Bridegroom is with them? As long as they have the Bridegroom with them, they cannot fast. But the days will come, when the Bridegroom shall be taken away from them, and then shall they fast in those days" (Ibid., 2:19-20).

The most beautiful verses regarding fasting are found in Matthew, the sixth chapter. Jesus said, "But thou, when thou fastest, anoint thine head, and wash thy face; that thou appear not unto men to fast, but unto Thy Father which is in secret: and Thy Father, which seeth in secret, shall reward thee openly" (Matt. 6:17-18). Folks, there will be a *reward* given for fasting, and it will be *openly* given; other people will see it.

Chapter Thirty-Two

A Hilarious Giver

There are many Scriptures regarding giving. Deuteronomy 16:16-17 states, "Three times in a year shall all thy males appear before the Lord thy God in the place which He shall choose; and they shall not appear before the Lord empty: every man shall give as he is able, according to the blessing of the Lord thy God which He hath given thee."

Jesus referred to a radical form of retribution when He said, "And if any man will sue thee at the law; and take away thy coat, let him have thy cloak also. And whosoever shall compel thee to go a mile, go with him twain. Give to him that asketh thee, and from him that would borrow of thee turn not away" (Matt. 5:40-42).

But then Christ followed with a promise of remuneration for such kind of sacrifices when He said, "Give, and it shall be given unto you; good measure, pressed down, and shaken together, and running over, shall men give into your bosom. For with the same measure that ye mete withal it shall be measured to you again" (Luke 6:38); and, "Give alms of such things as ye have; and, behold, all things are clean unto you" (Ibid., 11:41).

Paul preached: "I have shewed you all things, how that so labouring ye ought to support the weak, and to remember the words of the Lord Jesus, how He said, 'It is more blessed to give than receive'" (Acts 20:35); "Let him that stole steal no more: but rather let him labour, working with his hands the thing which is good, that he may have to give to him that needeth" (Eph. 4:28).

Paul told the proper attitude regarding giving when he wrote: "He that giveth, let him do it with simplicity" (Rom. 12:8); and, "But this I say, he which soweth sparingly shall reap also sparingly; and he which soweth bountifully shall reap bountifully. Every man according as he purposeth in his heart, so let him give: not grudgingly [Greek: sadness], or of necessity [Greek: distress]: for God loveth a cheerful giver" (2 Cor. 9:6-7).

The word "cheerful" in the preceding verse, used only once in the Bible, is the Greek word *hilaros*, from which we get the English word "hilarious." In other words, God loves hilarious givers—those who purpose how much they want to give, and then bestow it with a cheerful attitude, believing they are going to receive a reward for their giving!

Chapter Thirty-Three

The Shadow *Knows*

There are eighty references to shadows in the Bible. The book of Job mentions the most on the subject (seventeen), followed by David (fourteen), and then Isaiah (thirteen). The first time the word "shadow" crosses our path is in the book of Genesis.

Two angels, appearing in the form of men, came to visit Lot. They told him God was going to destroy Sodom, the city he was living in. Lot immediately invited them inside his home to eat. When perverse men of Sodom came and encircled Lot's residence, demanding that he bring the two strangers outside so they could sexually abuse them, Lot refused. He said, "Unto these men do nothing; for therefore came they under the shadow of my roof" (Gen. 19:8).

Job was a shadowy figure. He wrote: "As a servant earnestly desireth the shadow, and as an hireling looketh for the reward of his work: so am I made to possess months of vanity, and wearisome nights are appointed to me" (Job 7:2-3); and, "Who knoweth not in all these that the hand of the Lord hath wrought this? He discovereth deep things out of darkness, and bringeth out to light the shadow of death" (Ibid., 12:9, 22).

David also was a shady character. He directed: "Keep me as the apple of the eye, hide me under the shadow of Thy wings" (Ps. 17:6); "He that dwelleth in the secret place of the most High shall abide under the shadow of the Almighty" (Ibid., 91:1); "The Lord, is thy keeper: the Lord is thy shade upon thy right hand" (Ibid., 121:5); and,

"Such as sit in darkness and in the shadow of death, being bound in affliction and iron; because they rebelled against the words of God, and condemned the counsel of the most High: therefore He brought down their heart with labour; they fell down, and there was none to help. Then they cried unto the Lord in their trouble, and he saved them out of their distresses. He brought them out of darkness and the shadow of death, and brake their bands in sunder. Oh that men would praise the Lord for His goodness, and for His wonderful works to the children of men! (Ibid., 107:10-15)

Isaiah, not one to be kept in the shadows, wrote: "For Thou hast been a strength to the poor, a strength to the needy in his distress, a refuge from the storm, a shadow from the heat, when the blast of the terrible ones is as a storm against the wall" (Isa. 25:4);

"Behold a King shall reign in righteousness, and princes shall rule in judgment. And a man shall be as an hiding place from the wind, and a covert from the tempest; as rivers of water in a dry place, as a shadow of a great rock in a weary land" (Ibid., 32:1-2); and, "He hath made my mouth like a sharp sword; in the shadow of His hand hath He hid me, and made me a polished shaft; in His quiver hath He hid me" (Ibid., 49:2).

The Lord told Ezekiel, rather enigmatically,

I will also take of the highest branch of the high cedar, and will set it; I will crop off from the top of his young twigs a tender one, and will plant it upon an high mountain and eminent: in the mountain of the height of Israel will I plant it: and it shall bring forth boughs, and bear fruit, and be a goodly cedar: and under it shall dwell all fowl of every wing; in the shadow of the branches thereof shall they dwell. (Ezek. 17:22-23)

While Hosea held forth, "They that dwell under His shadow shall return; they shall revive as the corn and grow as the vine: the scent thereof shall be as the wine of Lebanon" (Hos. 14:7).

In the New Testament, Peter was so anointed that the

people, "brought forth the sick into the streets, and laid them on beds and couches, that at the least the shadow of Peter passing by might overshadow some of them" (Acts 5:15). Likewise, Paul commanded: "Let no man therefore judge you in meat, or in drink, or in respect of an holy day, or of the new moon, or of the Sabbath days: which are a shadow of things to come; but the body is of Christ" (Col. 2:16-17); and, "For the law having a shadow of good things to come, and not the very image of the things" (Heb. 10:1).

Jesus Christ heard that His relative, John the Baptist, was cast into prison. Because of what had happened to John, Christ left Nazareth and went to dwell in the seacoast town of Capernaum, which was in the borders of Zabulon and Nephtalim. There He fulfilled the prophecy of Isaiah: "The land of Zabulon, and the land of Nephtalim, by the way of the sea, beyond Jordan, Galilee of the Gentiles: the people which sat in the region and shadow of death light is sprung up" (Matt. 4:15-16).

When the "shadows of death" come—devastating disappointments, crushing calamities, flooring frustrations, bitter betrayals—the Lord will lighten your path with His shining Spirit.

Chapter Thirty-Four

Your Destiny Is Heads or Tails

It was in the first year after the children of Israel left the land of Egypt that Jethro, Moses' father-in-law, saw that Moses was judging the multitude of people by himself. He suggested that Moses enlist some help, which he did. Forty years later Moses recalled the event.

He said,

> I took the chief of your tribes, wise men, and known, and made them heads over you, captains over thousands, and captains over hundreds, and captains over fifties, and captains over tens, and officers among your tribes. And I charged your judges at that time, saying, "Hear the causes between your brethren, and judge righteously between every man and his brother, and the stranger that is with him. Ye shall not respect persons in judgment; but ye shall hear the small as well as the great; ye shall not be afraid of the face of man; for the judgment is God's: and the cause that is too hard for you, bring it unto me, and I will hear it." (Deut. 1:15-17)

In the second year after the children of Israel came out of the land of Egypt, God told Moses to number all the males 20-years-old* and upward, all who were "able to go to war"

---

*The draftable age was 20 years, instead of 18 as in the U.S.

(Num. 1:3). Then one man was chosen from every tribe. These men were, "the renowned of the congregation, princes of the tribes of their fathers, heads of thousands in Israel" (Num. 1:16). Thirty-nine years later, God made some incredible promises to all the Jews:

> The Lord shall open unto thee His good treasure, the heaven to give the rain unto thy land in his season, and to bless all the work of thine hand: and thou shalt lend unto many nations, and thou shalt not borrow. And the Lord shall make thee the head, and not the tail; and thou shalt be above only, and thou shalt not be beneath; if that thou hearken unto the commandments of the Lord thy God. (Deut. 28:12-13)

King David recognized that leadership was his true calling. He wrote, "Thou has delivered me from the strivings of the people; and Thou hast made me the head of the heathen: a people whom I have not known shall serve me. As soon as they hear of me, they shall obey me: the strangers shall submit themselves unto me" (Ps. 18:43-44).

The Hebrew word translated "head(s)" in the verses above is the same Hebrew word as "rulers" in: "Take you wise men, and understanding, and known among your tribes, and I will make them rulers over you" (Deut. 1:13); as "lead" in: "And it shall be, when the officers have made an end of speaking unto the people, that they shall make captains of the armies to lead the people" (Ibid., 20:9); as "chief" in: "And Abishai, the brother of Joab, the son of Zeruiah, was chief among three. And he lifted up his spear against three hundred, and slew them, and had the name among three" (2 Sam. 23:18); as "captains" in: "And they helped David against the band of the rovers: for they were all mighty men of valour, and were captains in the host" (1 Chron. 12:21); as "principal" in: "And Mattaniah the son of Micha, the son of Zabdi, the son of Asaph, was the principal to begin the thanksgiving in prayer" (Neh. 11:17); and, as "top" in: "But in the last days it shall come to pass, that the mountain of the house of the Lord shall be established in the top of the mountains, and it shall be exalted above the hills; and people shall flow unto it" (Micah 4:1).

It's divinely determined that every Christian ("spiritual Jew") climb to the "top" and become a "head" over men and women. All God requires you to do is observe His commandments. It's your destiny.

Chapter Thirty-Five

Dr. Patience

Patience is universally perceived as a beautiful characteristic. The Bible also recognizes it as a valuable trait. David, the first person in the Scriptures to use the word, dispensed: "Rest in the Lord, and wait patiently for Him: fret not thyself because of him who prospereth in his way, because of the man who bringeth wicked devices to pass" (Ps. 37:7); and, "I waited patiently for the Lord; and He inclined unto me, and heard my cry. He brought me up also out of an horrible pit, out of the miry clay, and set my feet upon a rock, and established my going" (Ibid., 40:1-2). Solomon also said, "the patient in spirit is better than the proud in spirit" (Eccles. 7:8). Amazingly, the three verses above are the *only* instances in the Old Testament where the word "patience" is mentioned.

The New Testament has a lot more to say on the subject. Jesus said that seed on the good ground, "are they, which in an honest and good heart, having heard the word, keep it, and bring forth fruit with patience" (Luke 8:15). The Master also manifested, "In your patience possess ye your souls" (Ibid., 21:19).

Paul said more about patience than any other biblical author, attesting: "Them who by patient continuance in well doing seek for glory and honour and immortality, eternal life" (Rom. 2:7); "We glory in tribulations also: knowing that tribulation worketh patience; and patience experience; and experience, hope" (Ibid., 5:3-4); "Truly the signs of an apostle were wrought among you in all patience, in signs, and wonders, and mighty deeds" (2 Cor. 12:12); "Be patient toward all men" (1 Thess. 5:14); "Follow after righteousness, godliness, faith, love, patience, meekness" (1 Tim. 6:11); "The servant of the Lord must not strive; but be gentle unto all men, apt to teach, patient" (2 Tim. 2:24); "Be not slothful, but followers of them who through faith and patience inherit the promises" (Heb. 6:12); "Ye have need of patience, that, after ye have done the will of God, ye might receive the promise" (Ibid., 10:36); and, "Seeing we also are compassed about with so great a cloud of witnesses, let us lay aside every weight, and the sin which doth so easily beset us, and let us run with patience the race that is set before us" (Ibid., 12:1).

Generalizations are not good to make, but I think most men would agree that women are more patient than men. James, the brother of Jesus, must have alluded to this when he wrote, "But let patience have her perfect work, that ye may be perfect and entire, wanting nothing" (James 1:4). James continued with: "Be ye also patient; stablish your hearts" (Ibid., 5:8); and,

> Take, my brethren, the prophets, who have spoken in the name of the Lord, for an example of suffering affliction and of patience. Behold, we count them happy which endure. Ye have heard of the patience of Job and have seen the end of the Lord; that the Lord is very pitiful, and of tender mercy. (Ibid., 5:10-11)

The Lord wants us to be patient, *because He is.* James wrote, "Be patient therefore, brethren, unto the coming of the Lord. Behold, the Husbandman waiteth for the precious fruit of the earth, and hath long patience for it, until He receive the early and latter rain" (James 5:7).

Peter punctuated, "For what glory is it, if, when ye be buffeted for your faults, ye shall take it patiently? But if, when ye do well, and suffer for it, ye take it patiently, this is acceptable with God" (1 Pet. 2:20); and then pointed out, "Now the God of patience and consolation grant you to be likeminded one toward another according to Christ Jesus" (Rom. 15:5).

Chapter Thirty-Six

The "All or Nothing" Rule

Moses was learned and in all the wisdom of the Egyptians, and was mighty in words in deeds. And when he was full forty years old, it came into his heart to visit his brethren the children of Israel. And seeing one of them suffer wrong, he defended him, and avenged him that was oppressed, and smote the Egyptian: *for he supposed his brethren would have understood how that God by his hand would deliver them: but they understood not.* (Acts 7:22-25; emphasis added)

Because Moses illegally killed the Egyptian who was oppressing a Jewish brother, he fled to the land of Midian to avoid prosecution by the Pharaoh. There, he stood up to some selfish shepherds who were keeping seven sisters from watering their father's flock. The grateful ladies took Moses home to meet their father. Exodus 2:21 states that, "Moses was content to dwell with the man." Forty years later Moses did, indeed, deliver the whole nation of Israel, but until then he had to be satisfied where he was.

David divulged, "The meek shall eat and be satisfied" (Ps. 22:26), while Solomon set down: "He that tilleth his land shall be satisfied with bread: but he that followeth vain persons is void of understanding" (Prov. 12:11); and, "He that loveth silver shall not be satisfied with silver; nor he that loveth abundance with increase" (Eccles. 5:10).

When soldiers came to John the Baptist and asked him what they were supposed to do, he told them, "Do violence to [intimidate] no man, neither accuse any falsely, and be content with your wages" (Luke 3:14).

Paul told the Philippian Christians,

> Not that I speak in respect of want: for I have learned, in whatsoever state I am, therewith to be content. I know both how to be abased, and I know how to abound: everywhere and in all things I am instructed both to be full and to be hungry, both to abound and to suffer need. I can do all things through Christ which strengtheneth me. (Phil. 4:11-13)

Then he added, "Let your conversation [behavior] be without covetousness; and be content with such things as ye have: for He hath said, 'I will never leave thee, nor forsake thee'" (Heb. 13:5).

There is something so satisfying about saving for a worthwhile goal (e.g., college education, ownership of a home, exotic vacation, etc.). The sacrifice made in such a pursuit can be likened to a state of "abasement" and the accomplishment of the same would be the condition of "abounding."

In whatever state we're in, whether involuntarily caused or self-imposed, Solomon gave wisdom when he declared, "In the day of prosperity be joyful, but in the day of adversity consider: God also hath set one against the other" (Eccles. 7:14).

Chapter Thirty-Seven

Thou Shalt Lend Unto Many Nations

The word loan is used only once in the Bible. The priest, Eli, referred to Hannah's son, Samuel, as a loan, lent to the Lord. Borrowing is referred to thirteen times, and lending nineteen times.

Various verses regarding "borrowing" are: "The children of Israel did according to the word of Moses; and they borrowed of the Egyptians jewels of silver, and jewels of gold, and raiment: and the Lord gave the people favor in the sight of the Egyptians, so that they lent unto them such things as they required" (Exod. 12:35-36); "And if a man borrow aught of his neighbor, and it be hurt, or die, the owner thereof being not with it, he shall surely make it good" (Ibid., 22:14); "The wicked borroweth, and payeth not again" (Ps. 37:21); "The borrower is servant to the lender" (Prov. 22:7); and, "Give to him that asketh thee, and from him that would borrow of thee turn not thou away" (Matt. 5:42).

Sundry Scriptures regarding lending are: "At the end of every seven years thou shalt make a release. And this is the manner of the release: Every creditor that lendeth aught unto his neighbor shall release it; he shall not exact it of his neighbor, or of his brother; because it is called the Lord's release" (Deut. 15:1-2); "If there be among you a poor man of one of thy brethren within any of thy gates in thy land which the Lord thy God giveth thee, thou shalt not harden thy heart, nor shut thine hand from thy poor brother: But thou shalt open thine hand wide unto him, and shalt surely lend him sufficient for his need, in that which he wanteth" (Ibid., 15: 7-8); "Unto a stranger thou mayest lend upon usury; but unto thy brother thou shalt not lend upon usury: that the Lord thy God may bless thee in all that thou settest thine hand to in the land whither thou goest to possess it" (Ibid., 23:20); "When thou dost lend thy brother anything, thou shalt not go into his house to fetch his pledge. Thou shalt stand abroad, and the man to whom thou dost lend shall bring out the pledge abroad unto thee" (Ibid., 24:11); "I have been young, and now am old; yet have I not seen the righteous forsaken nor his seed begging bread. He is ever merciful, and lendeth; and his seed blessed" (Psa. 37:25-26); "A good man sheweth favour, and lendeth: he will guide his affairs with discretion" (Ps. 112:5); "He that hath pity upon the poor lendeth unto the Lord; and that which he hath given will He pay him again" (Prov. 19:17); "And if ye lend to them of whom ye hope to receive, what thank have ye? For sinners also lend to sinners, to receive as much again. But love ye your enemies, and do good, and lend, hoping for nothing again, and your reward shall be great, and ye shall be the children of the Highest: for He is kind unto the unthankful and to the evil" (Luke 6:33-34).

The most important Scripture regarding borrowing and lending I saved for last. It is one of the greatest promises in the whole Bible: "The Lord shall open unto thee His good treasure, the heaven to give the rain unto thy land in His season and to bless all the work of thine hand: and thou shalt lend unto many nations, and thou shalt not borrow" (Deut. 28:12).

God wants His people to have financial security. There's only one stipulation that God put on this promise: "If that thou hearken unto the commandments of the Lord thy God, which I command thee this day, to observe and do them" (Ibid., 28:13).

Chapter Thirty-Eight

Don't Lose That Wait

The Bible promises many advantages to those who are willing to wait. David, who wrote more about the subject than anyone in the Bible, dispensed these words of wisdom:

"Wait on the Lord: be of good courage, and He shall strengthen thine heart: wait, I say, on the Lord" (Ps. 27:14); "Our soul waiteth for the Lord: He is our help and our shield" (Ibid., 33:20); "Those that wait upon the Lord, they shall inherit the earth" (Ibid., 37:9); "My soul, wait thou only upon God; for my expectation is from Him" (Ibid., 62:5); "Behold, as the eyes of the servants look unto the hand of their masters, and as the eyes of a maiden unto the hand of her mistress; so our eyes wait upon the Lord our God, until that He have mercy upon us" (Ibid., 123:2).

Isaiah instructed: "O Lord, be gracious unto us; we have waited for Thee: be Thou their arm every morning, our salvation in the time of trouble" (Isa. 33:2); "Even the youths shall faint and be weary, and the young men shall utterly fall: But they that wait upon the Lord shall renew their strength; they shall mount up with wings as eagles; they shall run, and not be weary; and they shall walk, and not faint" (Ibid., 40:30-31); and, "For since the beginning of the world men have not heard, nor perceived by the ear, neither hath the eye seen, O God, beside Thee, what He hath prepared for him that waiteth for Him" (Ibid., 64:4).

And Jeremiah joined with: "Are there any among the vanities of the Gentiles that can cause rain? Or can the heavens give showers? Art not Thou He, O Lord our God? Therefore we will wait upon Thee: for Thou hast made all these things" (Jer. 14:22); and,

"The Lord is good unto them that wait for Him, to the soul that seeketh Him. It is good that a man should both hope and quietly wait for the salvation of the Lord" (Lam. 3:25-26).

In the New Testament, Jesus told His disciples to, "wait for the promise of the Father, which," saith He, "ye have heard of Me" (Acts 1:4). And Paul, in referring to himself and others in the preaching profession, remarked, "let us wait on our ministering" (Rom. 12:7).

While we wait for our destinies to develop, we must remember that God is also waiting on us. For Isaiah illuminated, "And therefore will the Lord wait, that He may be gracious unto you, and therefore will He be exalted, that He may have mercy upon you: for the Lord is a God of judgment: blessed are all they that wait for Him" (Isa. 30:18).

Chapter Thirty-Nine

For Sheep's Sake

There are over 500 references to sheep and shepherds in the Bible. The very first reference to a lamb was in Genesis 22:7-8: "Isaac, spoke unto Abraham his father, and said, 'My father' and he said, 'Here am I, my son.' And he said, 'Behold the fire and the wood; but where is the lamb for a burnt offering?' And Abraham said, 'My son, God will provide Himself a lamb for a burnt offering.' "

In a prophecy of the coming Messiah, Isaiah wrote, "He shall feed His flock like a shepherd: He shall gather the lambs with His arm, and carry them in His bosom, and shall gently lead those that are with young" (Isa. 40:11). In a prophecy of the last days, Isaiah's words were, "The wolf and lamb shall feed together, and the lion shall eat straw like the bullock: and dust shall be the serpent's meat. They shall not hurt nor destroy in all My holy mountain, saith the Lord" (Ibid., 65:25).

Ezekiel wrote,

> For thus saith the Lord God; Behold, I, even I, will both search My sheep, and seek them out. As a shepherd seeketh out his flock in the day that he is among his sheep that are scattered; so will I seek out My sheep, and will deliver them out of all places where they have been scattered in the cloudy and dark day. (Ezek. 34:11-12)

Luke let us know: "Fear not, little flock; for it is your Father's good pleasure to give you the kingdom" (Luke 12:32);

and, "They overcame him [the great dragon] by the blood of the Lamb, and by the word of their testimony" (Rev. 12:11).

John wrote, "The next day John seeth Jesus coming unto him, and saith, 'Behold the Lamb of God, which taketh away the sin of the world'" (John 1:29). And Solomon wrote, "Be thou diligent to know the state of thy flocks, and look well to thy herds" (Prov. 27:23).

David, who had been a shepherd (1 Sam. 16:11), wrote one of the most beautiful pieces of prose, starting with:

> The Lord is my Shepherd; I shall not want. He maketh me to lie down in green pastures. He leadeth me beside the still waters. He restoreth my soul: He leadeth me in the paths of righteousness for His name's sake. Yea, though I walk through the valley of the shadow of death, I will fear no evil: for Thou art with me; Thy rod and Thy staff they comfort me. (Ps. 23:1-4)

After David was appointed king of Israel, he gained great insight to share with all leaders: "David perceived that the Lord had established him king over Israel, and that He had exalted his kingdom for His people Israel's sake" (2 Sam. 5:12). The Lord wants to raise up His people into positions of authority, because He knows they will act compassionately to the people He entrusts into their care.

And don't think because you've made mistakes in the past, you can't become a great leader. Look at Peter. He denied Jesus not once, but three times (Luke 22:55-61). After Jesus was resurrected He had dinner with His disciples. He asked Peter, "Simon, son of Jonas, lovest thou Me more than these?" Peter replied, "Yea, Lord; Thou knowest, that I love Thee." The Lord said to him, "Feed My lambs." He asked Peter a second time, "Simon, son of Jonas, lovest thou Me?" Peter again replied, "Yea, Lord; Thou knowest that I love Thee." Jesus again said, "Feed My sheep."

Jesus asked him one more time, "Simon, son of Jonas, lovest thou Me?" Peter was grieved because He had asked him the third time so he said to Him, "Lord, Thou knowest all things; Thou knowest that I love Thee." Jesus said, for the last time, "Feed My sheep" (John 21:15-17). Three denials, three declarations. Lo and behold, less than two months later, Peter preached the very first sermon of the Christian church!*

---

*Acts 2:14-39.

Chapter Forty

Join a Gym

In this age of athletics, there is a fervor for fitness, warm-ups, workouts, trainers and treadmills—the Bible is ever relevant. Paul wrote, "For bodily exercise profiteth [a]* little: but godliness is profitable unto all things, having promise of the life that now is, and of that which is to come" (1 Tim. 4:8).

I don't believe that Paul meant there was a "little" profit derived from physical exertion, but only that it was insignificant in comparison to the value derived from godliness. The Greek word for "exercise" in the above verse is *gymnasia* [training], from which we get our English word "gymnasium."

The Bible refers to many other types of exercise. David, in referring to his own self-effacing attitude, declared, "Lord, my heart is not haughty, nor mine eyes lofty: neither do I exercise myself in great matters, or in things too high for me" (Ps. 131:1).

Solomon, in commenting upon the futility of trying to find all the answers to life's questions, noted, "And I gave my heart to seek and search out by wisdom concerning all things that are done under heaven: this sore travail hath God given to the sons of man to be exercised therewith" (Eccles. 1:13).

---

*This "a" appears in the Greek manuscript.

The Lord, too, is "into" exercise. For He told Jeremiah, "I am the Lord which exercise lovingkindness, judgment, and righteousness in the earth: for in these things I delight, saith the Lord" (Jer. 9:24).

When two of Jesus' apostles asked to sit, one on His right and one on His left, in His glory, the other apostles got bent out of shape at the two glory-seekers. Jesus then said to them all,

> Ye know that they which are accounted to rule over the Gentiles exercise lordship over them; and their great ones exercise authority upon them. But so shall it not be among you: but whosoever will be great among you, shall be your minister: and whosoever of you will be the chiefest, shall be servant of all. For even the Son of man came not to be ministered unto, but to minister, and to give His life a ransom for many. (Mark 10:42-45)

Paul had to answer before Felix, the Roman governor of Judea, regarding certain charges made against him concerning his life and religious doctrine, and his response to the ruler was, "Herein do I exercise myself, to have always a conscience void of offense toward God, and toward men" (Acts 24:16).

Paul later used the Greek word *gymnazio* in two different contexts when writing to the Hebrew Christians. In the first instance, he admonished, "But strong meat [deep spiritual truths] belongeth to them that are of full age, even those who by reason of use have their senses exercised to discern both good and evil" (Heb. 5:12-14).

The second occasion is about correction from God: "For whom the Lord loveth He chasteneth, and scoureth every son He receiveth. Now no chastening for the present seemeth to be joyous, but grievous: nevertheless afterward it yieldeth the peaceable fruit of righteousness unto them which are exercised thereby" (Ibid., 12:6, 11).

Chapter Forty-One

The Body-God

Moses: "The Lord shall fight for you, and ye shall hold your peace" (Exod. 14:14).

Joshua: "One man of you shall chase a thousand: for the Lord your God, He it is that fighteth for you, as He hath promised you" (Josh. 23:10).

Hezekiah: "With us is the Lord our God to help us, and to fight our battles" (2 Chron. 32:8).

Nehemiah: "Our God shall fight for us" (Neh. 4:20).

David: "It is God that avengeth me, and subdueth the people under me" (Ps. 18:47).

Solomon: "Say not thou, 'I will recompense evil;' but wait on the Lord, and He shall save thee" (Prov. 20:22).

The Lord: "Thou shalt not avenge, nor bear any grudge against the children of thy people, but thou shalt love thy neighbour as thyself: I am the Lord" (Lev. 19:18).

The Lord wants to fight for us and He doesn't want us to take revenge on others. Paul pointed out: "Recompense to no man evil for evil" (Rom. 12:17); and, "avenge not yourselves, but rather give place [space] unto wrath: for it is written, 'Vengeance is Mine; I will repay, saith the Lord'" (Ibid., 12:19).

There is something that the Bible *expressly says* the Lord considers righteous: "It is a righteous thing with God to recompense tribulation to them that trouble you" (2 Thess. 1:6). In other words, God is waiting for the chance to take care of them who do you wrong—if you let Him.

The word translated "keep" in the Old Testament is a Hebrew word which means "to *hedge* about" (as with thorns), (i.e., to *guard)*. Examples: "O keep my soul, and deliver me: let me not be ashamed; for I put my trust in Thee" (Ps. 52:20). "Many are the afflictions of the righteous: but the Lord delivereth him out of them all. He keepeth all his bones: not one of them is broken" (Ibid., 34:19-20); "Except the Lord build the house, they labour in vain that build it: except the Lord keep the city, the watchman waketh but in vain" (Ibid., 127:1); "Keep me, O Lord, from the hands of the wicked; preserve me from the violent man; who have purposed to over-throw my goings" (Ibid., 140:4); "For the Lord shall be thy confidence, and shall keep thy foot from being taken" (Prov. 3:26); "He that scattered Israel will gather him, and keep him, as a shepherd doth his flock" (Jer. 31:10).

The Greek word most often translated "keep" in the New Testament means "to *watch,*" i.e., to *be on guard*. As in: "But the Lord is faithful, who shall stablish you, and keep you from evil" (2 Thess. 3:2); and, "Now unto Him that is able to keep you from falling, and to present you faultless before the presence of His glory with exceeding joy, to the only wise God our Saviour" (Jude 24-25).

When a great multitude came to arrest Jesus, Peter drew his sword and struck a servant of the high priest, slicing off the man's ear* (Matt. 26:51). Jesus then told Peter, "Put up again thy sword into his place: for all they that take the sword shall perish with the sword. Thinkest thou that I cannot now pray to My Father, and he shall presently give Me more than twelve legions of angels?"** (Ibid., 26:52-53).

If even Jesus did not defend Himself when He was doing the will of God, neither should we. Let the Body-God do it.

---

*Peter was probably aiming at the man's head and the intended target simply tried to duck out of the way.

**A Roman legion varied in number from 3000 to 6000 (so twelve legions would be between 36,000-72,000 angels).

Chapter Forty-Two

Two Are Better Than One

Pairs of people have accomplished great things in the Bible. Moses and his brother, Aaron, led over 2 million out of the land of Egypt (Exod. 12:31-37). Rachel and Leah "did build the house of Israel" (Ruth 4:11). Jonathan and his armorbearer defeated a garrison of the Philistines (1 Sam. 14:13-16). Jesus sent His disciples out by twos (Mark 6:7). Paul and Barnabas ministered together (Acts 15:36). Later, Paul hooked up with Silas to go to Syria, while Barnabas and Mark sailed over to Cyprus to preach (Ibid., 15:39-41).

Solomon wrote,

> Two are better than one; because they have a good reward for their labour. For if they fall, the one will lift up his fellow: but woe to him that is alone when he falleth; for he hath not another to help him up. Again, if two lie together, then they have heat: but how can one be warm alone? And if one prevail against him, two shall withstand him; and a threefold cord is not quickly broken. (Eccles. 4:9-12)

Jesus wrote, "Again, I say unto you, that if two of you shall agree on earth as touching any thing that they shall ask, it shall be done for them of My Father which is in heaven. For where two or three are gathered together in My name, there am I in the midst of them" (Matt. 18:19-20)!

To further illustrate this point, here is a small list of pairs of people who have founded well-known companies:

Al Neiman/Herman Marcus (Neiman-Marcus department stores)	Harley Procter/James Gamble (Procter and Gamble)
Henry Sherwin/Edward Williams (Sherwin-Williams paints)	Jack/Augustus Mack (Mack trucks)
Richard Sears/Alvah Roebuck (Sears and Roebuck)	Charles Rolls/Henry Royce (Rolls-Royce autos)
Burton Baskin/Irvine Robbins (Baskin-Robbins ice cream)	Duncan Black/Alonzo Decker (Black and Decker tools)
Steven/John Marriott (Marriott hotels)	William Hewlett/David Packard (Hewlett-Packard computers)
Richard/Maurice McDonald (McDonald's hamburgers)	Harry/Jack Warner (Warner Bros. Studio)
Andrew/William Smith (Smith Brothers Cough Drops)	Clarence/Edward Scott (Scott Paper)
James McDonald/Donald Douglass (McDonald-Douglas Aircraft)	Martin/John Bekins (Bekins Moving Company)
Charles Merrill/Edmund Lynch (Merrill Lynch)	Charles Dow/Edward Jones (Dow Jones)
Henry/Richard Block (H & R Block tax preparation)	William Wells/George Fargo (Wells Fargo)

The largest group of pairs of people in the world, however, capable of innumerable successful enterprises, is *husbands* and *wives*.

Chapter Forty-Three

Trial Twins

Abraham was 75-years-old when God told him, "I will make of thee a great nation" (Gen. 12:2,4). Later, Abraham reminded God that he was childless and, the way things stood, his only heir was going to be his house steward, Eliezer. The Lord then told Abraham, "He that shall come forth out of thine own bowels shall be thine heir" (Ibid., 15:4). The Bible then states that Abraham, "believed in the Lord; and He counted it to him for righteousness" (Ibid., 15:6).

Paul elaborated upon this point when he told the Christians in Rome:

> Who against hope believed in hope, that he might become the father of many nations, according to that which was spoken, "So shall they seed be." And being not weak in faith, he considered not his own body now dead, when was about an hundred years old, neither yet the deadness of Sarah's womb: he staggered not at the promise of God through unbelief; but was strong in faith, giving glory to God; and was fully persuaded that, what He had promised, He was able to perform. (Rom. 4:18-21)

Comparing Genesis 12:4 with Romans 4:19, we see that Abraham ended up waiting twenty-five years before his promised son, Isaac, was born (Gen. 21:5). It's no wonder Paul wrote of the patriarch, "Therefore it is of faith, that it might be by grace; to the end the promise might be sure to all the seed;

not to that only which is of the law, but to that also which is of the faith of Abraham; who is the father of us all" (Rom. 4:16).

The Bible doesn't say how old Abraham was when he married Sarah, but it does record the age of his son, Isaac. He was, "forty years old when he took Rebekah to wife" (Gen. 25:20). The Bible then reveals an interesting fact about Isaac and Rebekah.

Verse 21 of the same chapter states, "And Isaac intreated the Lord for his wife, because she was barren: and the Lord was intreated of him, and Rebekah his wife conceived." The Bible then relates that when Rebekah was wondering about the unusual activity in her womb, she inquired of the Lord. God told her that she was carrying twin boys and that each would become a great nation.

So far, the only similarity between the marital experiences of Abraham and Isaac is the fact that both wives were barren. That is, until you read Genesis 25:26. There it tells that Esau was born first. Then, "came his brother out, and his hand took hold on Esau's heel; and his name was called Jacob: and Isaac was *threescore* years old when she bare them" (italics added).

The impact of the end of this verse has probably escaped the notice of a lot of Bible enthusiasts. Verse 20 states that Isaac was 40-years-old when he got married, and verse 26 discloses that he was threescore-years-old when his barren wife bore twins. "Threescore" is Old Testament lingo for sixty years.* In other words, Isaac prayed to God for twenty years (five years less than his father, Abraham) before God answered his prayer!

The fact that Isaac went through almost the exact same trial as his father was to Isaac's advantage in at least three ways: (1) It appears, by historical records, to be the major trial of Isaac's life, which he passed successfully; (2) His father went through almost the identical experience so he was able to give Isaac wise counsel in how to deal with it; and (3) Isaac didn't

---

*A "score" is twenty years.

have any children by another woman, so he didn't have a "problem child" like his dad did.

Isaac underwent another incident similar to his father. Abraham's wife, at 90-years-old, was still so beautiful that he lied to King Abimelech of Gerar and said she was his sister. He thought the ruler was going to slay him to get his wife (Gen. 20:11). When there was another famine in the land during Isaac's marriage, he also moved to Gerar. He told the men there that Rebekah was his sister, for he was afraid to say, "'She is my wife,' lest the men of the place kill him for Rebekah, "because she was fair to look upon" (Ibid., 26:7).

Though both Sarah and Rebekah went through trials over their barrenness, each experienced the same blessing—they were able to retain their exceptional beauty well into old age!

Chapter Forty-Four

Ten Thousand Percent Profit

In the Bible, there are sixty-eight references to profit and ninety-two references to prosperity:

"In all labour there is profit" (Prov. 14:23); "Moreover the profit of the earth is for all: the king himself is served by the field" (Eccles. 5:9); "If iron be blunt, and he do not whet the edge, then must he put to more strength: but wisdom is profitable to direct" (Ibid., 10:10); "I am the Lord thy God which teacheth to profit, which leadeth thee by the way that thou shouldest go" (Isa. 48:17); "Even as I please all men in all things, not seeking mine own profit, but the profit of many, that they may be saved" (1 Cor. 10:33); "The manifestation of the Spirit is given to every man to profit withal" (Ibid., 12:7); "All Scripture is given by inspiration of God, and is profitable for doctrine, for reproof, for correction, for instruction in righteousness" (2 Tim. 3:16); "That they which have believed in God might be careful to maintain good works. These things are good and profitable unto men" (Titus 3:8); "And the Lord was with Joseph, and he was a prosperous man" (Gen. 39:2); "Keep therefore the words of this covenant, and do them, that ye may prosper in all that ye do" (Deut. 29:9); "Yea, let them say continually, 'Let the Lord be magnified, which hath pleasure in the prosperity of His servant' "(Ps. 35:27); "O Lord, I beseech Thee, send now prosperity" (Ibid., 118:25); and "Beloved, I wish above all things that thou mayest prosper and be in health, even as thy soul prospereth" (3 John 2).

There was a famine in the land during the time of Isaac, so he went to Gerar, in the land of the Philistines. When he had been there a long time, Genesis 26:12 relates that "Isaac sowed in the land, and received in the same year an hundredfold: and the Lord blessed him." The term "hundredfold" means "one hundred times" an amount (not 100 *percent,* which would only be twice as much). To put it another way, God's percentage of profit is 10,000 percent!

To show that God's formula applies not only to agricultural crops, let's go to the New Testament. Peter said to the Lord, "Lo, we have left all, and have followed Thee." Jesus replied,

> Verily I say unto you, There is no man that hath left house, or brethren, or sisters, or father, or mother, or wife, or children, or lands, for My sake, and the gospel's, but he shall receive an hundredfold now in this time, houses, and brethren, and sisters, and mothers, and children, and lands, with persecutions: and in the world to come eternal life. (Mark 10:29-30)

Chapter Forty-Five

Cast Your Cares into the Air

It came to pass that Jesus entered into a certain village where a woman named Martha received Him into her house. She had a sister, Mary, who sat at Jesus' feet and listened to Him speak. Martha, who was cumbered about with much serving, went to Jesus and said, "Lord, dost Thou not care that my sister hath left me to serve alone? Bid her therefore that she help me" (Luke 10:38-40).

Jesus answered and said to her, "Martha, Martha, thou art careful and troubled about many things: but one thing is needful: and Mary hath chosen that good part, which shall not be taken away from her" (Ibid., 10:41-42).

The word "careful" that Jesus used is King James English for "full of *worry*"* (and not cautious or thorough). The same Greek word is used in Philippians 4:6, where Paul wrote, "Be careful for nothing; but in every thing by prayer and supplication with thanksgiving let your requests be made known unto God."

Again, it's the root of the same Greek word for "careful" that's translated "thought" in Matthew 6:25-34, where Jesus said:

---

*The words "anxious," "anxiety," and "worry" do not appear in the KJV Bible.

Therefore I say unto you, Take no thought for your life, what ye shall eat, or what ye shall drink; nor yet for your body, what ye shall put on. Is not the life more than meat, and the body than raiment? Behold the fowls of the air: for they sow not, neither do they reap, nor gather into barns; yet your heavenly Father feedeth them. Are ye not much better than they? Which of you by taking thought can add one cubit unto his stature? And why take ye thought for raiment? Consider the lilies of the field, how they grow: they toil not, neither do they spin: And yet I say unto you, that even Solomon in all his glory was not arrayed like one of these. Wherefore, if God so clothe the grass of the field, which to day is, and to morrow is cast into the oven, shall he not much more clothe you, O ye of little faith? Therefore take no thought saying, What shall we eat? Or, what shall we drink? Or, wherewithal shall we be clothed? (For after all these things do the Gentiles seek:) for your heavenly Father knoweth that ye have need of all these things. But seek ye first the kingdom of God, and His righteousness; and all these things shall be added unto you. Take therefore no thought for the morrow: for the morrow shall take thought for the things of itself. Sufficient unto the day is the evil thereof.

In the book of Luke, Jesus said, "When they bring you unto the synagogues, and unto magistrates, and powers, take ye no thought how or what ye shall say: for the Holy Ghost shall teach you in the same hour what ye ought to say" (Luke 12:11-12). Again, the Greek word for *worry* is used.

So how does one get rid of worries? Saint Peter gave the answer. He wrote, "Casting all your care upon Him; for He careth for you" (1 Pet. 5:7). The secret to shedding stress, alleviating anxiety, or unburdening uneasiness is to believe that Christ loves you and wants to take your troubles!

Chapter Forty-Six

The Profit of Prayer

Abraham's wife, Sarah, at 99 years of age, was so beautiful that Abraham told a half truth—essentially, a lie. He told King Abimelech that Sarah was his sister* because he was afraid the ruler would kill him to get his wife (Gen. 20:11). God, however, told Abimelech the truth in a dream after he had, as Abraham had feared, schemed on Sarah.

The Lord then told Abimelech that Abraham would have to pray for him. In what was to be the first prayer recorded in the Bible, "Abraham prayed unto God: and God healed Abimelech, and his wife, and his maidservants; and they bare children. For the Lord had fast closed up all the wombs of the house of Abimelech, because of Sarah, Abraham's wife" (Gen. 20:17-18).

After Solomon and the people concluded construction of the temple, the king kneeled and delivered one of the longest prayers in the Bible, twenty-nine verses.** When Solomon finished praying, fire came down from heaven and consumed the sacrifice of *22,000* oxen and *120,000* sheep!

---

*She was really his half-sister, as they both had the same father (Gen. 20:12).

**2 Chronicles 6:14-42. (Compare: Jesus' prayer in the seventeenth chapter of John was 26 verses.)

Later, the Lord appeared to Solomon by night and told him He had heard his prayer. God then promised: "If My people, which are called by My name shall humble themselves, and pray, and seek My face, and turn from their wicked ways; then will I hear from heaven, and will forgive their sin, and will heal their land" (2 Chron. 7:14).

At the end of Job's trial, the Lord expressed His anger toward Job's three friends, Eliphaz, Elihu, and Bildad. The Lord told them,

> Therefore take unto you now seven bullocks and seven rams, and go to My servant Job, and offer up for yourselves a burnt offering; and My servant Job shall pray for you: for Him will I accept: lest I deal with you after your folly, in that ye have not spoken of Me the thing which is right, like My servant Job. (Job 42:8)

After the three "miserable comforters" did what the Lord commanded, the Bible states that, "the Lord also accepted Job. And the Lord turned the captivity of Job, when he prayed for his friends: also the Lord gave Job twice as much as he had before" (Ibid., 42:9-10).

David said: "The Lord hath heard my supplication; the Lord will receive my prayer" (Ps. 6:9); "For this shall every one that is godly pray unto Thee in a time when Thou mayest be found: surely in the floods of great waters they shall not come nigh unto him" (Ibid., 32:6); and, "He will regard the prayer of the destitute, and not despise their prayer" (Ibid., 102:17).

When King Hezekiah was sick unto death, he turned his face to the wall and prayed, "Remember now, O Lord, I beseech Thee, how I have walked before Thee in truth and with a perfect heart, and have done that which is good in Thy sight." After he finished praying he wept profusely (Isa. 38:2-3). The word of the Lord then came to Isaiah and told him to say to Hezekiah, "Thus saith the Lord, the God of David thy father, I have heard thy prayer, I have seen thy tears: behold, I will add unto thy days fifteen years" (Ibid., 38:4-5).

Later, the Lord told Isaiah,

> Also the sons of the stranger, that join themselves to the Lord, to serve Him, and to love the name of the Lord, to be His servants, every one that keepeth the Sabbath from polluting it, and taketh hold of My covenant; even them will I bring to My holy mountain, and make them joyful in My house of prayer. (Isa. 56:6-7)

The Lord also told Jeremiah, "Seek the peace of the city whither I have caused you to be carried away captives, and pray unto the Lord for it: for in the peace thereof shall ye have peace" (Jer. 29:7).

The Lord prophesied to Zechariah, "It shall yet come to pass, that there shall come people, and the inhabitants of many cities: and the inhabitants of one city shall go to another, saying, 'Let us go speedily to pray before the Lord, and to seek the Lord of hosts: I will go also.' Yea, many people and strong nations shall come to seek the Lord of hosts in Jerusalem, and to pray before the Lord" (Zech. 8:20-22).

Jesus said, "Therefore I say unto you, what things soever ye desire, when ye pray, believe that ye receive them, and ye shall have them" (Mark 11:24). The Lord also gave us a model prayer:

> Our Father which art in heaven, hallowed be Thy name. Thy kingdom come. Thy will be done in earth, as it is in heaven. Give us this day our daily bread. And forgive us our debts, as we forgive our debtors. And lead us not into temptation, but deliver us from evil: for Thine is the kingdom, and the power, and the glory, for ever. Amen. (Matt. 6:9-13)

Paul wrote, "For every creature of God is good, and nothing to be refused, if it be received with thanksgiving: for it is sanctified by the word of God and prayer" (1 Tim. 4:4-5). James joined with,

> Is any sick among you? Let him call for the elders of the church; and let them pray over him, anointing him with oil in the name of the Lord: and the prayer of faith

shall save the sick, and the Lord shall raise him up; and
if he have committed any sins, they shall be forgiven
him. (James 5:14-15)

This final verse stands alone, both in its reasonable expectation of privacy and its promise of profit: "But thou, when
thou prayest, enter into thy closet, and when thou hast shut the
door, pray to Thy Father which is in secret; and Thy Father
which seeth in secret shall reward thee openly" (Matt. 6:6).

Chapter Forty–Seven

Put a Knife to Your Throat

Bosses are the modern-day equivalents of the kings of old. King Solomon gave some timeless advice that can apply to current relationships with bosses and board members, supervisors and superiors, presidents and principals. The son of David declared:

1. "In the multitude of people is the king's honour: but in the want of people is the destruction of a prince" (Prov. 14:28). Translation: *Always side with management.*

2. "The king's favour is toward a wise servant: but his wrath is against him that causeth shame" (Ibid., 14:35). Translation: *Don't embarrass your employer.*

3. "Righteous lips are the delight of kings; and they love him that speaketh right" (Ibid., 16:13). Translation: *Don't lie to a leader.*

4. In the light of the king's countenance is life; and his favour is as a cloud of the latter rain" (Ibid., 16:15). Translation: *Make your superior smile.*

5. "The fear of a king is as the roaring of a lion: whoso provoketh him to anger sinneth against his own soul" (Ibid., 20:2). Translation: *Don't make your manager mad.*

6. "A king that sitteth in the throne of judgment scattereth away all evil with his eyes" (Ibid., 20:8). Translation: *Don't try to deceive your director.*

7. "He that loveth pureness of heart, for the grace of his lips the king shall be his friend" (Ibid., 22:11). Translation: *Talk sincerely with tact.*

8. "The heaven for height, and the earth for depth, and the heart of kings is unsearchable" (Ibid., 25:3). Translation: *Don't try to figure out a foreman.*

9. "Take away the wicked from before the king, and his throne shall be established in righteousness" (Ibid., 25:5). Translation: *Do wrong, and you'll be fired.*

10. "Put not forth thyself in the presence of the king, and stand not in the place of great men: for better it is that it be said unto thee, 'Come up hither'; than that thou shouldest be put lower in the presence of the prince whom thine eyes have seen" (Ibid., 25:6-7). Translation: *Don't praise yourself.*

11. "Many seek a ruler's favour; but every man's judgment cometh from the Lord" (Ibid., 29:26). Translation: *Don't always ask authorities for things.*

12. "I counsel thee to keep the king's commandment, and that in regard of the oath of God" (Eccles. 8:2). Translation: *Obey orders.*

13. "Where the word of a king is, there is power: and who may say unto him, 'What doest thou?' " (Ibid., 8:4). Translation: *Don't question your director's decisions.*

14. "Curse not the king, no not in thy thought; and curse not the rich in thy bedchamber: for a bird of the air shall carry the voice, and that which hath wings shall tell the matter" (Ibid., 10:20). Translation: *Don't bad-mouth your boss, even in private.*

15. "When thou sittest to eat with a ruler, consider diligently what is before thee: and put a knife to thy throat, if thou be a man given to appetite. Be not desirous of his dainties" (Prov. 23:1-3). Translation: *Watch what you say and don't entertain gossip.*

Chapter Forty–Eight

Dream Makers

There are over 100 references to dreams in the Bible, the first being: "God came to king Abimelech in a dream by night" and warned him that the woman he had taken unto himself was Abraham's wife (Gen. 20:3).

Jacob dreamed and saw "a ladder set upon the earth, and the top of it reached to heaven: and behold the angels of God ascending and descending on it" (Ibid., 28:12). Twenty years later, in another dream, he saw rams and cattle that, "were ringstraked, speckled and grisled" (Ibid., 31:10). When Jacob fled Laban, his father-in-law, God appeared to Laban in a dream, and told him, "Take heed that thou speak not to Jacob either good or bad" (Ibid., 31:24).

The Lord appeared to Solomon in a dream by night and said to him, "Ask what I shall give thee" (1 Kings 3:5). Nebuchadnezzar had a dream at night, forgot it when he woke up, and Daniel miraculously discerned the dream and its interpretation (Dan. 2). Nebuchadnezzar had another dream, which he remembered, and Daniel again interpreted it (Ibid., 4). Then Daniel had a dream himself (Ibid., 7) and an angel told him the interpretation!

An angel appeared to Joseph, in a dream, and told him not to fear to take Mary as his wife, for the Child in her was of the Holy Ghost (Matt. 1:20). Again, he was warned of God in a dream to go back to their country a different way because Herod wanted to kill him (Ibid., 2:12). Then, as he was departing, an angel appeared to Joseph in a dream and told him to take his family to Egypt (Ibid., 2:13). When Herod was dead, an angel appeared to Joseph in a dream and told him and his family to go back to the land of Israel (Ibid., 2:19-20). When Joseph heard that Herod's son reigned in his father's stead, he was afraid to go back. But after being warned of God in a dream he dwelt in a town called Nazareth (Ibid., 2:22-23). With five recorded dreams to his credit, Joseph heads the list.

In the book of Joel, God said,

> And it shall come to pass afterward, that I will pour out My Spirit upon all flesh; and your sons and daughters shall prophesy, your old men shall dream dreams, your young men shall see visions: and also upon the servants and upon handmaids in those days will I pour out My Spirit. (Joel 2:28-29)

When Joseph was 17-years-old he told his brothers this dream: "Behold, we were binding sheaves in the field, and, lo, my sheaf arose, and also stood upright; and behold, your sheaves stood round about, and made obeisance to my sheaf" (Gen. 37:7). His brothers hated him because of the dream. Joseph dreamed again that the sun, moon, and stars bowed down to him. His brothers hated him even more, and even his father rebuked him (Ibid., 37:9-10).

Joseph's dreams came to pass, after he helped others fulfill their dreams. After his brothers sold Joseph into slavery, he ended up overseeing all the possessions of his master, Potiphar. The Lord even blessed the Egyptian officer for Joseph's sake (Ibid., 39:1-6). When Joseph was falsely accused by Potiphar's wife and thrown into prison, he accurately interpreted the dreams of the butler and baker (Ibid., 40:12-20). Two years later Joseph correctly interpreted a dream of the Pharaoh and afterwards was made a ruler in the country. Whenever Joseph's chariot passed by, the people cried before him, "Bow the knee" (Ibid., 41:43).

Do dreams come to those who merely sleep a lot, or spend a lot of time meditating or staring off into space? Not according to the Bible. Solomon said, "Love not sleep, lest thou come to poverty" (Prov. 20:13). Solomon also shared this secret of success: "A dream cometh through a multitude of business" (Eccles. 5:3). In other words, God gives dreams to busy, industrious people. Jesus confirmed this when He said, "For I say unto you, that unto every one which hath shall be given; and from him that hath not even that he hath shall be taken away from him" (Luke 19:26).

Chapter Forty-Nine

Endurance Records

All successful leaders (biblical or otherwise) endured many things before their goals were accomplished. Though King Saul and his soldiers chased David around the countryside trying to kill him (Saul threw a javelin at David on two separate occasions*), David endured until, eventually, he replaced Saul as king. Joseph was betrayed by his brothers, sold into slavery, falsely accused, and imprisoned. He endured for thirteen years** until his boyhood dream was fulfilled.

Paul pressed us to, "endure hardness as a good soldier of Jesus Christ" (2 Tim. 2:3). He spoke from personal experiences because he reported, seven verses later, "I endure all things for the elects' sakes, that they may also obtain the salvation which is in Christ Jesus with eternal glory."

Apostle James wrote encouragingly, "Behold, we count them happy which endure. Ye have heard of the patience of Job, and have seen the end of the Lord; that the Lord is very pitiful, and of tender mercy" (James 5:11). Job 42:12 explains what the "end of the Lord" was: "The Lord blessed the latter end of Job more than his beginning: for he had fourteen thousand sheep, and six thousand camels, and a thousand yoke of oxen,

---

*1 Samuel 18:11 and 19:10
**Compare Genesis 37:2 with 41:46

and a thousand she asses." When compared to the list of live-stock in 1:3, we see that Job truly received twice as much as what he had before—all because he endured!

Paul declared: "When God made promise to Abraham, because He could swear by no greater, He sware by Himself, saying, 'Surely blessing I will bless thee, and multiplying I will multiply thee.' And so, after he had patiently endured, he obtained the promise" (Heb. 6:13-15); and, "Despise not the chastening of the Lord, nor faint when thou art rebuked of Him: for whom the Lord loveth He chasteneth, and scourgeth every son whom He receiveth. If ye endure chastening, God dealteth with you as with sons; for what son is he whom the father chasteneth not?" (Ibid., 12:5-7).

So, *how* does one endure? I believe that love is the key. First Corinthians 13, the love chapter, reveals that, "charity* suffereth long and is kind; beareth all things, believeth all things, hopeth all things, endureth all things" (1 Cor. 13:4, 7). Paul proved that love could endure all things when he provided, "persecutions I endured: but out of them all the Lord delivered me" (2 Tim. 3:11). In conclusion, Christ mentioned an endurance record that all Christians hope to set: "He that endureth to the end shall be saved" (Matt. 10:22).

---

*Greek: *agape* (love).

Chapter Fifty

Lover of Truth

There are over 300 references to truth in the Bible. In the Old Testament, almost every time the Hebrew word is used it means: "stability." In the New Testament, in almost every instance the Greek word which is used means: "not hidden." Selected Scriptures regarding truth include:

"Thy word is true from the beginning" (Ps. 119:160); "A true witness delivereth souls" (Prov. 14:25); "He that hath received His testimony hath set to his seal that God is true" (John 3:33); "The true worshippers shall worship the Father in Spirit and truth" (Ibid., 4:23); "The Son of God is come, and hath given us an understanding, that we may know Him that is true, and we are in Him that is true, even in His son Jesus Christ. This is the true God, and eternal life" (1 John 5:20);

"He that walketh uprightly, and worketh righteousness and speaketh the truth in his heart . . . He that doeth these things shall never be moved" (Ps. 15:2, 5); "Lead me in thy truth, and teach me" (Ibid., 25:5); "All the paths of the Lord are mercy and truth unto such as keep His covenant and His testimonies" (Ibid., 25:10); "Thou hast redeemed me, O Lord God of truth" (Ibid., 31:5); "For the word of the Lord is right; and all His works are done in truth" (Ibid., 33:4); "For Thy mercy is great unto the heavens, and Thy truth unto the clouds" (Ibid., 57:10);

"Truth shall spring out of the earth; and righteousness shall look down from heaven" (Ibid., 85:11); "His truth shall be thy shield and buckler" (Ibid., 91:4); "His truth endureth to all generations" (Ibid., 100:5); "Thou art near, O Lord; and all Thy commandments are truth" (Ibid., 119:51); "The Lord is nigh unto all them that call upon Him, to all that call upon Him in truth" (Ibid., 145:18); "Let not mercy and truth forsake thee: bind them about thy neck; write them upon the table of thine heart: so shall thou find favour and good understanding in the sight of God and man" (Prov. 3:3);

"He that speaketh truth sheweth forth righteousness" (Ibid., 12:17); "The lips of truth shall be established forever" (Ibid., 12:19); "Mercy and truth shall be to them that devise good" (Ibid., 14:22); "Have not I written to thee excellent things in counsels and knowledge, that I might make thee know the certainty of the words of truth; that thou mightest answer the words of truth to them that send unto thee?" (Ibid., 22:21); "Buy the truth and sell it not" (Ibid., 23:23); "They shall be My people, and I will be their God, in truth and in righteousness" (Zech. 8:8); "And ye shall know the truth, and the truth shall make you free" (John 8:32); "Jesus saith unto him, 'I am the way, the truth, and the life'" (Ibid., 14:6);

"When He, the Spirit of truth, is come, He will guide you into all truth: for He shall not speak of Himself" (Ibid., 16:13); "Sanctify them through Thy truth: Thy word is truth" (Ibid., 17:17); "Speak every man truth with his neighbour" (Eph. 4:25); "The fruit of the Spirit is in all goodness and righteousness and truth" (Ibid., 5:9); "God our Saviour; who will have all men to be saved, and to come unto the knowledge of the truth" (1 Tim. 2:3-4); "The house of God, which is the church of the living God, the pillar and ground of the truth" (Ibid., 3:15); and, "Of His own will begat He us with the word of truth, that we should be a kind of first fruits of His creatures" (James 1:18).

To "be saved," one must simply be a lover of truth (2 Thess. 2:10).

Chapter Fifty-One

Dust Off Your Shoes

There are over 93 references to dust in the Old Testament, beginning with: "The Lord God formed man of the dust of the ground, and breathed into his nostrils the breath of life; and man became a living soul" (Gen. 2:7).

While pleading with God not to destroy Sodom and Gomorrah (undoubtedly because his nephew lived there), Abraham said, "Behold now, I have taken upon me to speak unto the Lord, which am but dust and ashes" (Ibid., 18:27). The Lord later assured Abraham, "And thy seed shall be as the dust of the earth, and thou shalt spread abroad to the west, and to the east, and to the north, and to the south: and in thee and in thy seed shall all the families of the earth be blessed" (Ibid., 28:14).

Job wrote, "As for the earth, out of it cometh bread: and under it is turned up as it were fire. The stones of it are the place of sapphires: and it hath dust of gold" (Job 28:5-6). When God showed Job just some of His creative credentials, Job groveled. "I abhor myself, and repent in dust and ashes" (Ibid., 42:6), Job declared.

David discoursed: "Like a father pitieth his children, so the Lord pitieth them that fear Him. For He knoweth our frame; He remembereth that we are dust" (Ps. 103:13-14); and, "He raiseth up the poor out of the dust, and lifteth the needy out of the dunghill; that He may set him with princes, even with the princes of His people" (Ibid., 113:7-8).

Isaiah, in describing the magnitude of God, inquired, "Who hath measured the waters in the hollow of His hand, and meted out heaven with the span, and comprehended the dust of the earth in a measure, and weighed the mountains in scales, and the hills in a balance?" (Isa. 40:12).

There are only seven references to dust in the New Testament. Five of them deal with the same set of facts as recorded in the ninth and tenth chapters of Luke*:

> And He said unto them, "Take nothing for your journey, neither staves, nor scrip, neither bread, neither money; neither have two coats apiece. And whatsoever house ye enter into, there abide, and thence depart. And whosoever will not receive you, when you go out of that city, shake off the very dust from your feet for a testimony against them." (Luke 9:3-5)

> But whatsoever city ye enter, and they receive you not, go your ways out into the streets of the same, and say, "Even the very dust of your city, which cleaveth on us, we do wipe off against you: notwithstanding be ye sure of this, that the kingdom of God is come nigh unto you." (Luke 10:10-11)

Whether it be your manuscript, musical masterpiece, invention, or inspirational idea, if those to whom you have submitted your material reject it, shake their dust off your feet! Don't get discouraged. They are not simply worthy of your work! God has provided a better thing for you!**

---

*The other four are Matthew 10:14, Mark 6:11, Luke 10:11, and Acts 13:51.

**Hebrews 11:39-40

Chapter Fifty-Two

Ravishing Romance

Marital bliss is alive and well according to the Bible. The earliest reference to marriage is: "Therefore shall a man leave his father and mother, and shall cleave unto his wife: and they shall become one flesh. And they were both naked, the man and his wife, and were not ashamed" (Gen. 2:24-25). (Most translations render the word "cleave" in the verse above as "cling.")

On his honeymoon night, Isaac consorted with Rebekah, "and she became his wife; and he loved her: and Isaac was comforted after his mother's death" (Ibid., 24:67). When Isaac was 60-years-old the Philistine king, Abimelech, looked out a window and saw Isaac "sporting with Rebekah" (Ibid., 26:8). The overwhelming majority of translations render "sporting" as either "fondling" or "caressing." Isaac was still captivated by his wife after twenty years of marriage.

Solomon stated: "Whoso findeth a wife findeth a good thing, and obtaineth favour of the Lord" (Prov. 18:22); and "live joyfully with the wife whom thou lovest all the days of thy life" (Eccles. 9:9). But where Solomon really got descriptive is in the Song of Solomon, where the Preacher* wrote, lyrically:

---

*Seven times Solomon is referred to as "the Preacher": Ecclesiastes 1:1, 1:2, 1:12, 7:27, 12:8, 12:9, and 12:10.

Behold, thou art fair, my love; behold, thou art fair;
thou hast doves' eyes within thy locks: thy hair is as a
flock of goats, that appear from mount Gilead. Thy
teeth are like a flock of sheep that are even [ly] shorn,
which came up from the washing; wherein every one
bear twins, and none is barren among them. Thy lips
are like a thread of scarlet, and thy speech is comely:
thy temples are like a piece of a pomegranate within thy
locks. Thy neck is like the tower of David builded for
an armoury, whereon there hang a thousand bucklers,
all shields of mighty men. Thy two breasts are like two
young roes that are twins, which feed among the lilies.
(Song of Solomon 4:1-5)

Apostle Paul, though he never married, had great insight
into marital matters. He wrote, "So ought men to love their
wives as their own bodies. He that loveth his wife loveth himself. For no man ever yet hated his own flesh; but nourisheth
and cherisheth it" (Eph. 5:28-29). So should men nourish and
cherish their wives.

Paul pleaded with the wives, "submit yourselves unto your
own husbands, as unto the Lord" (Ibid., 5:22). This is a verse
that I'm sure a lot of Christian husbands know about (only too
well). But are the same husbands also aware of the commandment to them which, I believe, is harder to implement than the
submission requirement is to women? It is: "Husbands love
your wives, even as Christ loved the church, and gave Himself
for it" (Ibid., 5:25).

Hebrews 13:4 states that, "marriage is honorable [Greek:
valuable, costly] in all and the bed undefiled [Greek: *pure*]." In
other words, in marriage anything goes! The Greek word for
honorable in this verse is the same word translated "honour" in:
"Likewise, ye husbands, dwell with them according to knowledge giving honour unto the wife" (1 Pet. 3:7).

Solomon's wife wrote, "the king hath brought me into his
chambers: we will be glad and rejoice in thee, we will remember thy love more than wine" (Song of Solomon 1:4). The
Hebrew word for "love" here means "to *boil*." Is this hot stuff
or what?

This discussion can best be capped off by what Solomon wrote: "Let thy fountain be blessed: and rejoice with the wife of thy youth. Let her be as the loving hind and pleasant roe; let her breasts satisfy thee at all times; and be thou ravished with her love" (Prov. 5:18-19).

One translation renders "satisfy" in the preceding verse variously as: "delight" (*New Jerusalem Bible*). Other translations render "ravished" variously as: "captive" (*New Jerusalem Bible*); "exhilarated" (*New American Standard*); "transported with delight" (*Amplified*); and "captivated" (*New International Version*).

Remember this: the created being can't possess a greater degree of romance than its Creator. Christ, our Lord, is the consummate Lover!

Chapter Fifty-Three

An Abundant Life

There are over 900 references to life and living in the Bible. Moses mentioned: "The tree of the field is man's life" (Deut. 20:19); and "Choose life, that both thou and thy seed may live: that thou mayest love the Lord thy God, and that thou mayest cleave unto Him: for He is thy life, and length of days" (Ibid., 30:19-20).

David declaimed: "Thou wilt shew me the path of life" (Ps. 16:11); "Take fast hold of instruction; let her not go: keep her; for she is thy life" (Prov. 4:13); "In the way of righteousness is life" (Ibid., 12:28); "A sound heart is the life of the flesh" (Ibid., 14:30); and "The fear of the Lord tendeth to life: and he that hath it shall abide satisfied" (Ibid., 19:23).

The Gospels give us: "For He is not a God of the dead, but of the living: for all live unto Him" (Luke 20:38); "In Him was life; and the life was the light of men" (John 1:4); "For as the Father hath life in Himself; so hath He given to the Son to have life in Himself" (Ibid., 5:26); "Like as Christ was raised up from the dead by the glory of the Father, even so we also should walk in newness of life" (Rom. 6:4); "For now we live, if we stand fast in the Lord" (1 Thess. 3:8); and "Godliness is profitable unto all things, having promise of the life that now is, and of that which is to come" (1 Tim. 4:8).

John wrote: "God sent His only begotten Son into the world, that we might live through Him" (1 John 4:9); and, "He that hath the Son hath life" (Ibid., 5:12).

But Jesus Christ didn't come to bring *only* life, for He said, "I am come that they might have life and that they might have it more abundantly" (John 10:10). The Greek word translated "abundantly" in this verse is the same word that is rendered, "abundance" in: "For whosoever hath, to him shall be given, and he shall have more abundance" (Matt. 13:12).

It's also the same Greek word translated "measure" in Mark 6. In that chapter it tells about Jesus walking on the water. Verse 50 states that when the apostles all saw Him, they "were troubled." When Christ joined them in their ship, the wind ceased. The apostles were then, "sore amazed in themselves beyond measure" (Mark 6:51).

The abundant life that Christ offers is so beyond the measure we could set for ourselves that it is truly amazing!

Chapter Fifty-Four

A Musing Thought to Success

To "muse" means to *meditate*—both words are used interchangeably in the Old Testament. The first reference to meditation is in Genesis. Isaac's mother died and his father, Abraham, sent the family's most trusted servant to procure a wife for his son. Isaac "went out to meditate in the field at the eventide: and he lifted up his eyes, and saw, and, behold, the camels were coming. And Rebekah [his bride-to-be] lifted up her eyes, and when she saw Isaac, she lighted off her camel" (24:63-64).

Of the twenty-three references to meditation in the Bible, David wrote seventeen, including:

"But his delight is in the law of the Lord; and in His law doth he meditate day and night. And he shall be like a tree planted by the rivers of water, that bringeth forth his fruit in his season; his leaf also shall not wither; and whatsoever he doeth shall prosper" (Ps. 1:2-3); "Give ear to my words, O Lord, consider my meditation" (Ibid., 5:1); "Let the words of my mouth, and the meditation of my heart, be acceptable in Thy sight, O Lord, my strength, and my Redeemer" (Ibid., 19:14);

"My heart was hot within me, while I was musing the fire burned: then spake I with my tongue, 'Lord, make me to know mine end, and the measure of my days, what it is; that I may know how frail I am'" (Ibid., 39:3-4); "The meditation of my heart shall be of understanding" (Ibid., 49:3); "My soul shall be

satisfied as with marrow and fatness; and my mouth shall praise
Thee with joyful lips: when I remember Thee upon my bed,
and meditate on Thee in the night watches" (Ibid., 63:5-6); "I
will meditate also of all Thy work, and talk of Thy doings"
(Ibid., 77:12);

"My meditation of Him shall be sweet: I will be glad in the
Lord" (Ibid., 104:34); "I will meditate in Thy precepts, and
have respect unto Thy ways" (Ibid., 119:15); "Princes also did
sit and speak against me: but Thy servant did meditate in Thy
statutes" (Ibid., 119:23); "Oh how love I Thy law! It is my
meditation all the day" (Ibid., 119:97); "I have more understanding than all my teachers: for Thy testimonies are my
meditation" (Ibid., 119:99); and, "I remember the days of old;
I meditate on all Thy works; I muse on the work of Thy hands"
(Ibid., 143:5).

The New Testament records that the followers of John the
Baptist, "were in expectation, and all men mused in their hearts
of John, whether he were the Christ, or not" (Luke 3:15). John
then assured his disciples that he was not the Messiah.

Jesus told the people what they should do when they were
brought before kings or rulers for His sake. He said, "Settle it
therefore in your hearts, not to meditate before what ye shall
answer: for I will give you a mouth and wisdom, which all your
adversaries shall not be able to gainsay nor resist" (Ibid., 21:14-
15). And Paul told Timothy, "give attendance to reading, to
exhortation, to doctrine . . . meditate upon these things; give
thyself wholly to them; that thy profiting may appear to all" (1
Tim. 4:13, 15).

The most beneficial Scripture regarding meditation, however, is in the book of Joshua. After the death of Moses, the
Lord spoke to Joshua, his successor, and promised him, "This
book of the law shall not depart out of thy mouth; but thou
shalt meditate therein day and night, that thou mayest observe
to do according to all that is written therein: for then thou shalt
make thy way prosperous, and then thou shalt have good success" (Josh. 1:8). It is worth noting that this is the only time in
the Bible that the word "success" is mentioned.

Chapter Fifty-Five

Looking for a Leader?
Try the Infirmary

There are twenty-two references to infirmities in the Bible, only three of which are located in the Old Testament. David, feeling forsaken, declared,

> Will the Lord cast off for ever? And will He be favourable no more? Is His mercy clean gone for ever? Doth His promise fail for evermore? Hath God forgotten to be gracious? Hath He in anger shut up His tender mercies? Selah. And I said, "This is my infirmity: but I will remember the years of the right hand of the most High." (Ps. 77:7-10)

Paul, telling the Hebrew Christians about the compassion of Christ, wrote, "For we have not an High Priest which cannot be touched with the feeling of our infirmities; but was in all points tempted like as we are, yet without sin" (Heb. 4:15).

Paul suffered with a "thorn in the flesh"* (2 Cor. 4:7). When the Lord would not remove it after Paul had sought

---

*The Bible doesn't say what the "thorn" was, but some scholars believe it was his poor eyesight, because he wrote to the church at Galatia, "I bear you record, that, if it had been possible, ye would have plucked out your own eyes, and have given them to me" (Gal. 4:15); and, "see what large letters I use as I write" (Ibid., 6:11, NIV).

Him three times, the prophet then pledged, "Most gladly therefore will I glory in my infirmities, that the power of Christ may rest upon me. Therefore I take pleasure in infirmities, in reproaches, in necessities, in persecutions, in distresses for Christ's sake: for when I am weak, then am I strong" (2 Cor. 12:10). In an earlier book he said, "the Spirit also helpeth our infirmities" (Rom. 8:26).

Paul once told the churches at Rome, "But God be thanked, that ye were the servants of sin, but ye have obeyed from the heart that form of doctrine which was delivered you. Being then made free from sin, ye became the servants of righteousness" (Ibid., 6:17-18). Then he added, "I speak after the manner of men because of the infirmity of your flesh" (Ibid., 6:19). And, toward the end of the same book, he stated, "We then that are strong ought to bear the infirmities of the weak, and not to please ourselves" (15:1).

It's in the book of Hebrews, however, that Paul dropped a bombshell, declaring, "For every high priest taken from among men is ordained in things pertaining to God, that he may offer both gifts and sacrifices for sins. Who can have compassion on the ignorant, and on them that are out of the way; for he himself also is compassed with infirmity" (Heb. 5:1-2).

I believe Paul reveals that God purposely chooses people with "infirmities" (e.g., poor self-image, low personal esteem, shyness, nervousness, compulsive behavior, oversensitiveness, etc.,) to be leaders. Thus, being aware of their own limitations and shortcomings, they are able to "Deal gently with those who are ignorant and are going astray" (Ibid., *New International Version*); "Deal gently with the ignorant and misguided" (Ibid., *New American Standard*); and, "Exercise gentleness and forbearance toward the ignorant and erring" (Ibid., *Amplified Bible*).

Chapter Fifty-Six

Fear Is a Paper Lion

Fifteen times in the New Testament Jesus said, "Fear not."* He knew that humans are, at times, susceptible to various kinds of fears. The Greek word that the Lord used was *phobos*, from which we get the English word "phobia." You might be surprised to learn that great men in the Bible also experienced various kinds of fear.

Isaac lied and said that his wife was his sister. He was afraid the Philistines would kill him because his wife was, "fair to look upon" (Gen. 26:7). Jacob feared that his brother would kill him, his wife, and children because many years before he had stolen his brother's birthright (Ibid., 32:11). Job said that what he had "greatly feared" had come upon him (Job 3:25). David feared reproach (Ps. 119:39). Apostle Paul said that within him were fears (2 Cor. 7:5), and Apostle Peter feared what the Jews would think of him because he had eaten with the Gentiles (Gal. 2:12).

There are, according to the Bible, at least three ways to eliminate fears:

---

*Mt. 1:20, 10:28, 10:31, 28:5, Lk. 1:13, 1:30, 2:10, 5:10, 8:50, 12:7, 12:32, 18:4, Jn. 12:15, Acts 27:24, Rev. 1:17

1. Perfect Love–Apostle John wrote that, "there is no fear in love; but perfect love casteth out fear: because fear hath torment" (1 John 4:18). "Perfect," as used here, is the Greek word *teleios*, which means "complete."*

    Regarding perfect love, John also wrote that if we keep God's word, "the love of God is perfected" (Ibid. 2:5); and, "if we love one another, God dwelleth in us, and His love is perfected in us" (Ibid. 4:12).

2. Seeking the Lord–King David wrote, "I sought the Lord, and He heard me, and delivered me from all my fears" (Ps. 34:4).

    In addition to delivering from fears, seeking the Lord has other advantages:

    (a) "They that seek the Lord shall not want any good thing" (Ps. 34:10);

    (b) "Your heart shall live that seek God" (Ibid. 69:32);

    (c) "They that seek the Lord understand all things" (Prov. 28:5).

3. Before I tell you the third way to eliminate fear, I would like to start off talking about sloths. A sloth is a four-legged mammal, in the same order as armadillos and anteaters, that moves slowly as it hangs upside down from branches. The word "slothful" is used to describe a lazy person, as is the word "sluggard," from where we get the word slug, a slimy snail.

    The Bible lists twenty-three Scriptures dealing with sloths and sluggards, such as: "The hand of the diligent shall bear rule: but the slothful shall be under tribute" (Prov. 12:24); "The slothful man roasteth not that which he took in hunting" (Ibid., 12:27); "The way of the slothful man is a hedge of thorns" (Ibid., 15:19); "He also that is slothful in work is brother to him that is a great waster" (Ibid., 18:9);

---

*It is where we get the English word "telesis," a sociological term defined as the utilization of the processes of nature and society to obtain particular goals.

"The desire of the slothful killeth him; for his hands refuse to labour" (Ibid., 21:25); "As the door turneth upon his hinges, so doth the slothful upon his bed" (Ibid., 26:14); "Slothfulness casteth into a deep sleep; and an idle soul shall suffer hunger" (Ibid., 19:15); "By much slothfulness the building decayeth; and through idleness of the hands the house droppeth through" (Eccles. 10:18);

"Go to the ant, thou sluggard; consider her ways, and be wise: which having no guide, overseer, or ruler provideth her meat in the summer, and gathereth her food in the harvest" (Prov. 6:6-8); "The soul of the sluggard desireth, and hath nothing" (Ibid., 13:4); "The sluggard will not plow by reason of the cold; therefore shall he beg in harvest, and have nothing" (Ibid., 20:4); and, "The sluggard is wiser in his own conceit than seven men that can render a reason" (Ibid., 26:16).

What does the study of sloths and sluggards have to do with extinguishing fear? The answer lies in Proverbs 22:13, which states, "The slothful man saith, 'There is a lion without, I shall be slain in the streets.' " The lazy man used fear as an excuse not to work. Because his mind was idle, fear had been able to enter into it.

So you see, the third way to eliminate fear is the opposite of slothfulness: industriousness. Fear is caused by unproductive thoughts. Since the mind can only focus on one thing at a time, we must keep our minds busy with productive thoughts.

The Staff of Life

A staff (a stick or rod used either as a support or symbol of authority) is mentioned in various circumstances in the Scriptures. Jacob said to the Lord, "I am not worthy of the least of all the mercies, and of all the truth, which thou hast shewed unto Thy servant; for with my staff I passed over this Jordan; and now I am become two bands [of people]" (Gen. 32:10).

In instituting the Passover, the Lord told Moses, "And thus shall ye eat it; with your loins girded, your shoes on your feet, and your staff in your hand; and ye shall eat it in haste: it is the Lord's Passover" (Exod. 12:11).

In describing the giant Goliath, Samuel stated that, "the staff of his spear was like a weaver's beam" (1 Sam. 17:7). David, before he confronted the giant, "took his staff in his hand, and chose him, five smooth stones out of the brook" (Ibid., 17:40). Later, when David was king, one of his mighty men, Elhanan, "slew the brother of Goliath the Gittite"* (2 Sam. 21:19). The staff of his spear was also the size of a weaver's beam.

Benaiah, another of David's mighty men, came against an Egyptian warrior of great stature and, "went down to him with a staff, and plucked the spear out of the Egyptian's hand, and

---

*An inhabitant of Gath.

slew him with his own spear" (1 Chron. 11:23). In his well-known twenty-third Psalm, David wrote, "Yea, though I walk through the valley of the shadow of death, I will fear no evil: for Thou art with me; Thy rod and Thy staff they comfort me" (Ps. 23:4).

The Lord, referring to the audacity of His people rebelling against Him, said, "Shall the axe boast itself against him that heweth therewith? Or shall the saw magnify itself against him that shaketh it? As if the rod should shake itself against them that lift it up, or as if the staff should lift up itself, as if it were no wood" (Isa. 10:15).

When Jesus sent out His twelve disciples, He said unto them, "Take nothing for your journey, neither staves, nor scrip, neither bread, neither money; neither have two coats apiece. And whosoever house ye enter into, there abide, and thence depart" (Luke 9:3-4). Later, when a multitude came to arrest Jesus, He said to the chief priests and captains of the temple, "Be ye come out, as against a thief, with swords and staves?" (Ibid., 22:52).

When Moses told the Lord that the people would not believe that God had sent him, the Lord said to him, "What is in thine hand?" Moses replied, "A rod."* The Lord then told him to cast it on the ground. When he did so, it became a serpent and Moses fled from it (Exod. 4:2-3).

The Lord then told Moses, "Put forth thine hand, and take it by the tail." When he did so it became a rod in his hand. The Lord told Moses, "That they may believe that the Lord God of their fathers, the God of Abraham, the God of Isaac, and the God of Jacob, hath appeared unto thee" (Ibid., 4:4-5).

Every one of us has a staff in our hand—i.e., talents, abilities, gifts, etc. If we turn them over to the Lord, each will become like a staff of life to feed the multitudes.

*Hebrew: a *branch* (fig. a staff).

Chapter Fifty-Eight

Infinite Understanding

Though we all want to be understood by those we admire it is better to understand ourselves and others. The Psalmist proclaimed: "The meditation of my heart shall be of understanding" (Ps. 49:3); "Man that is in honour, and understandeth not, is like the beasts that perish" (Ibid., 49:20); "A good understanding have all they that do His commandments" (Ibid., 111:10); "I have more understanding than all my teachers: for thy testimonies are my meditation" (Ibid., 119:99); and, "The entrance of Thy words giveth light; it giveth understanding unto the simple" (Ibid., 119:130).

Solomon said: "With all thy getting get understanding" (Prov. 4:7); "In the lips of him that hath understanding wisdom is found" (Ibid., 10:13); "Good understanding giveth favour" (Ibid., 13:15); "He that is slow to wrath is of great understanding" (Ibid., 14:29); "The heart of him that hath understanding seeketh knowledge" (Ibid., 15:14); "Understanding is a wellspring of life unto him that hath it" (Ibid., 15:22); "He that keepeth understanding shall find good" (Ibid., 19:8).

"Counsel in the heart of man is like deep water; but a man of understanding will draw it out" (Ibid., 20:5); "For the transgression of a land many are the princes thereof: but by a man of understanding and knowledge the state thereof shall be prolonged" (Ibid., 28:2); "Evil men understand not judgment: but they that seek the Lord understand all things" (Ibid., 28:5); and, "The rich man is wise in his own conceit; but the poor that hath understanding searcheth him out" (Ibid., 28:11).

Paul wrote: "That which is known of God is manifest in them; for God hath shewed it unto them. For the invisible things of Him from the creation of the word are clearly seen, being understood by the things that are made, even His eternal power and Godhead" (Rom. 1:19-20); and,

"That their hearts might be comforted, being knit together in love, and unto all riches of the full assurance of understanding, to the acknowledgment of the mystery of God, and of the Father, and of Christ; in whom are hid all the treasures of wisdom and knowledge" (Col. 2:2-3).

Job, who went through wearisome tribulation, wrote thoroughly,

> Whence then cometh wisdom? And where is the place of understanding? Seeing it is hid from the eyes of all the living, and kept close from the fowls of the air. Destruction and death say, "We have heard the fame thereof with our ears." God understandeth the way thereof, and He knoweth the place thereof. For He looketh to the ends of the whole earth, and seeth under the whole heaven; to make the weight for the winds; and He weigheth the waters by measure. When He made a decree for the rain, and a way for the lightning and thunder: then did He see it, and declare it; He prepared it, yea, and searched it out. And unto man He said, "Behold, the fear of the Lord, that is wisdom; and to depart from evil is understanding." (Job 28:20-28)

When trying times, excruciating events, difficult days come, and you desperately desire to talk to someone who truly understands, read Psalms 147:5: "Great is our Lord, and of great power: His understanding is infinite."

Chapter Fifty-Nine

If God Repented, So Can We

"God *repent*? How could that be? He's never sinned!"* Didn't Samuel say, "The strength of Israel will not lie nor repent: for He is not a man, that He should repent?"** Well, God not only promised He *would* repent,*** but it's recorded, on at least twelve separate occasions, that He did so.

The first reference to God repenting is Genesis 6:6: "it repented the Lord that He had made man on the earth," because his thoughts were only evil continually. Moses pleaded with God when He wanted to consume the children of Israel for their wickedness, and, "the Lord repented of the evil which He thought to do unto His people" (Exod. 32:14);

When the Lord raised up judges throughout Israel, then, "the Lord was with the judge, and delivered them out of the hand of their enemies all the days of the judge: for it repented the Lord because of their groanings by reason of them that oppressed them and vexed them" (Judg. 2:18).

Because Saul transgressed the commandment of the Lord because he obeyed the voice of the people instead of the voice of God, "the Lord repented that He had made Saul king over Israel" (1 Sam. 15:35).

---

*2 Corinthians 5:21
**1 Samuel 15:29
***Psalms 135:14, Jeremiah 18:8, 10; 26:3, 13.

Many times the Lord delivered His people. He, "regarded their affliction, when He heard their cry: and He remembered for them His covenant, and repented according to the multitude of His mercies" (Ps. 106:44-45).

The king of Nineveh proclaimed a fast and decreed that neither man nor beast could eat or drink anything and that every man and beast had to be covered with sackcloth. God saw their works and, "repented of the evil, that He had said He would do unto them; and He did it not" (Jonah 3:10).

In the New Testament, Jesus said, "Repent ye, and believe the gospel" (Mark 1:15); Peter preached, "Repent, and be baptized every one of you in the name of Jesus Christ for the remission of sins" (Acts 2:38); Paul pronounced, "the goodness of God leadeth thee to repentance" (Rom. 2:4); and, "godly sorrow worketh repentance to salvation not to be repented of" (2 Cor. 7:10).

If God isn't too great to repent, who are we to think that we don't need to?

Chapter Sixty

Have a Beautiful Time

The Bible mentions a lot about things of beauty (over 100 references), while the word "ugly" is not mentioned once. The Scriptures elaborate on beauty with: "Rachel was beautiful and well favoured" (Gen. 29:17); "Abigail: and she was a woman of good understanding, and of a beautiful countenance" (1 Sam. 25:3); "The woman was very beautiful to look upon. And David sent and inquired after the woman. And one said, 'Is not this Bathsheba . . . ?' " (2 Sam. 11:3); "And he brought up Hadassah, that is, Esther, his uncle's daughter: for she had neither father nor mother, and the maid was fair and beautiful" (Esther 2:7); "Thou art beautiful, O my love, as Tirzah, comely as Jerusalem" (Song of Solomon 6:4); "And it came to pass, before, he had done speaking, that, behold, Rebekah came out and the damsel was very fair* to look upon" (Gen. 24:15, 16); "So they sought for a fair damsel throughout all the coasts of Israel, and found Abishag a Shunammite, and brought her to the king. And the damsel was very fair, and cherished the king, and ministered to him" (1 Kings 1:3-4); and "And in all the land were no women found so fair as the daughters of Job" (Job 42:15).

---

*The Hebrew word for "fair" in this context is the same Hebrew word used for "beautiful."

Abram's wife, Sarai, was so beautiful at 65-years-old* that the Pharaoh of Egypt tried to take her as his wife! "And it came to pass, that when Abram was come into Egypt, the Egyptians beheld the woman that she was very fair. The princes also of Pharaoh saw her, and commended her before Pharaoh" (Gen. 12:14-15).

Not every beautiful woman is virtuous, however. Solomon instructed:

"For the commandment is a lamp; and the law is light; and reproofs of instruction are the way of life: to keep thee from the evil woman, from the flattery of the tongue of a strange woman. Lust not after her beauty in thine heart; neither let her take thee with her eyelids" (Prov. 6:23-25); "As a jewel of gold in a swine's snout, so is a fair woman which is without discretion" (Ibid., 11:22); and, "Favour is deceitful, and beauty is vain: but a woman that feareth the Lord, she shall be praised" (Ibid., 31:30).

Isaiah 61:1-3 foretold particulars of the ministry of the Messiah (Jesus later quoted two of the first three verses):

> The Spirit of the Lord God is upon Me: because the Lord hath anointed Me to preach good tidings unto the meek; He hath sent Me to bind up the broken-hearted, to proclaim liberty to the captives, and the opening of the prison to them that are bound; to proclaim the acceptable year of the Lord, and the day of vengeance of our God; to comfort all that mourn; to appoint unto them that mourn in Zion, to give unto them beauty for ashes, the oil of joy for mourning, the garment of praise for the spirit of heaviness.

Yes, Christ came so this Old Testament Scripture might be fulfilled: "He hath made everything beautiful in His time" (Eccles. 3:11).

---

*Sarai was ten years younger than her husband (Gen. 17:17), and at the time of this incident Abraham was 75-years-old (Gen. 12:4).

Chapter Sixty-One

More Thoughts Than the Sand

Sand is made up of tiny loose grains of rocks or minerals. The most common mineral found in sand is quartz. Grains of sand vary in size from $1/12$ of an inch to smaller than $1/400$ of an inch in diameter, and it takes *millions* of grains of sand to fill one cup!

There are twenty-eight references to sand in the Bible. Most of them use a simile (a figure of speech in which two dissimilar things are compared) and/or hyperbole (extravagant exaggeration not to be taken literally).

The Lord told Abraham,

> That in blessing I will bless thee, and in multiplying I will multiply thy seed as the stars of the heaven, and as the sand which is upon the sea shore; and thy seed shall possess the gate of his enemies; and in thy seed shall all the nations of the earth be blessed; because thou hast obeyed my voice. (Gen. 22:17-18)

During the seven years of plenty in Egypt, "Joseph gathered corn as the sand, very much, until he left numbering; for it was without number" (Ibid., 41:49).

When Moses blessed the people of Israel before he died, he said to two tribes, "Rejoice, Zebulun, in thy going out; and, Issachar, in thy tents. They shall call the people unto the mountain; there they shall offer sacrifices of righteousness: for they shall suck of the abundance of the seas, and of the treasures hid in the sand" (Deut. 33:18-19).

First Kings 4:29 states that, "God gave Solomon wisdom and understanding exceeding much, and largeness of heart, even as the sand that is on the sea shore."

Job, during his great trial, said, "Oh that my grief were thoroughly weighed, and my calamity laid in the balances together! For now it would be heavier than the sand of the sea" (Job 6:1-2). While Solomon wrote, "A stone is heavy, and the sand weighty; but a fool's wrath is heavier than them both" (Prov. 27:3).

In a prophecy foretelling the vast numbers of Israelite people and ministers of the gospel that were going to exist in the future, the Lord said, "As the host of heaven cannot be numbered, neither the sand of sea measured: so will I multiply the seed of David My servant, and the Levites that minister unto Me" (Jer. 33:22).

The most singular reference to sand, however, reveals how much God thinks about us! For David said: "How precious also are Thy thoughts unto me, O God! How great is the sum of them! If I should count them, they are more in number than the sand: when I awake, I am still with Thee" (Ps. 139:18).

Chapter Sixty-Two

Convert to a Child

Regarding the category of children, David said: "He shall judge the poor of the people, He shall save the children of the needy" (Ps. 72:4); "As a father pitieth his children, so the Lord pitieth them that fear Him" (Ibid., 103:13); "The mercy of the Lord is from everlasting to everlasting upon them that fear Him, and His righteousness unto children's children" (Ibid., 103:17);

"Lo, children are an heritage of the Lord: and the fruit of the womb is His reward. As arrows are in the hand of a mighty man; so are children of the youth. Happy is the man that hath his quiver full of them" (Ibid., 127:3-5); and, "Thy wife shall be as a fruitful vine by the sides of thine house: thy children like olive plants round about thy table. Behold, that thus shall the man be blessed that feareth the Lord. Yea, thou shalt see thy children's children, and peace upon Israel" (Ibid., 138:3-4, 6).

On the same subject Solomon specified: "Children's children are the crown of old men; and the glory of children are their fathers" (Prov. 17:6); "The just man walketh in his integrity: his children are blessed after him" (Ibid., 20:7); "Even a child is known by his doings, whether his work be pure, and whether it be right" (Ibid., 20:11); "Train up a child in the way he should go: and when he is old, he will not depart from it" (Ibid., 22:6); and, "The father of the righteous shall greatly rejoice: and he that begetteth a wise child shall have joy of him" (Ibid., 23:24).

Paul, though he never married, had keen insight into children. He counseled: "Children, obey your parents in the Lord: for this is right" (Eph. 6:1); "Ye fathers, provoke not your children to wrath: but bring them up in the nurture and admonition of the Lord" (Ibid., 6:4); "Children, obey your parents in all things: for this is well pleasing unto the Lord" (Col. 3:20);

"Let the deacons be the husbands of one wife, ruling their children and their own houses well" (1 Tim. 3:12); "Ordain elders in every city, as I had appointed thee: if any be blameless, the husband of one wife, having faithful children not accused of riot or unruly" (Titus 1:6); and, "Teach the young women to be sober, to love their husbands, to love their children" (Ibid., 2:4).

Five times in one chapter, Apostle John used the phrase "little children," including: "My little children, these things write I unto you, that ye sin not" (1 John 2:1); "I write unto you, little children, because your sins are forgiven you for His name's sake" (Ibid., 2:12); "I write unto you, little children, because ye have known the Father" (Ibid., 2:13); "And now, little children, abide in Him" (Ibid., 2:28).

Christ loved children. When His disciples were arguing about who was the greatest in heaven, Jesus called forth a little child and set him in the midst of the disciples. Then He said, "Verily I say unto you, except ye be converted, and become as little children, ye shall not enter the kingdom of heaven. Whosoever therefore shall humble himself as this little child, the same is the greatest in the kingdom of heaven. And whoso shall receive one such little child in My name receiveth Me" (Matt. 18:3-5).

The Greek word translated as "converted" in the second sentence of the preceding paragraph is the Greek word *strepho*, "to turn quite around," from which we get our English words "*strepto*coccus"* ("strep" throat) and "*strepto*mycin."** The Lord wants us to use the "streptomycin" of conversion to heal the diseases of our souls.

---

*Any of various spherical bacteria; some cause serious diseases.
**An antibiotic drug used to treat various diseases.

Chapter Sixty-Three

Thou Shalt Provide for Thine Own Family

Abraham was, "very rich in cattle, in silver, and in gold" (Gen. 13:2). Lot, Abraham's nephew, was also well off, as his "substance was great" (Ibid., 13:6). Later, Abraham, "gave all that he had unto Isaac" his son (Ibid., 25:5).

Boaz, David's grandfather, was "a mighty man of wealth" (Ruth 2:1). Job's substance, "was seven thousand sheep, and three thousand camels, and five hundred yoke of oxen, and five hundred she asses, and a very great household"; he "was the greatest of all the men of the east" (Job 1:3).

David had "treasures," "storehouses in the fields, in the cities, and in the villages," and "castles" (1 Chron. 27:25), while his son, Solomon, "exceeded all the kings of the earth for riches" (1 Kings 10:23). Because, "the Lord stablished the kingdom in his hand," Jehoshaphat had, "riches and honour in abundance" (2 Chron. 17:5).

There is much detail in the Bible regarding the personal fortune of King Hezekiah. He had,

> Exceeding much riches and honour: and he made himself treasuries for silver, and for gold, and for precious stones, and for spices, and for shields, and for all manner of precious jewels; storehouses also for the increase of corn, and wine, and oil; and stalls for all manner of beasts, and cotes for flocks. Moreover He provided him cities, and possessions of flocks and herds in abun-

dance: for God had given him substance very much.
(Ibid., 32:27-29)

Josiah also had so much wealth that he, "gave to the people, of the flock, lambs and kids, all for the Passover offerings, for all that were present, to the number of thirty thousand, and three thousand bullocks: these were of the king's substance" (Ibid., 35:7). Joseph, the disciple who begged for the body of Jesus and laid Him to rest in his own tomb, was "a rich man of Arimathaea" (Matt. 27:57).

We can assume, from the descriptions of assets of the men mentioned above, that they were able to provide for their own families. It is no surprise, then, that Apostle Paul pronounced, "But if any provide not for his own, and specially for those of his own house, he hath denied the faith, and is worse than an infidel" (1 Tim. 5:8). The Greek word translated "provide," here means "to consider in advance, look out for beforehand" (by way of maintenance of others).

So, if God is requiring us to provide for our own families, doesn't it make sense that since it's His commandment, He wants to help us do it in such a way that He gets great glory?

Chapter Sixty-Four

The Force Stay with You

Force is used in a variety of ways in the Scriptures. When Jacob and his family fled from Laban, his father-in-law, and Laban caught up with them, Jacob told his father-in-law why he ran. He said, "Because I was afraid: for I said, 'Peradventure Thou wouldest take by force thy daughters from me' " (Gen. 31:31).

Job said, "How forcible are right words!" And, in referring to the toll being taken upon his body, commented, "By the force of my disease is my garment changed: it bindeth me about as the collar of my coat" (Ibid., 30:18).

Solomon, in describing the influence an adulterous woman has upon a young man void of understanding, summoned, "With much fair speech she caused him to yield, with the flattering of lips she forced him" (Prov. 7:21).

In a prophecy heralding the coming of salvation to the Gentile people, Isaiah wrote, "Therefore thy gates shall be open continually; they shall not be shut day nor night; that men may bring unto thee the forces of the Gentiles, and that their kings may be brought" (Isa. 60:11).

Because of all the false prophets in the land, Jeremiah wrote, "For all the land is full of adulterers; for because of swearing the land mourneth; the pleasant places of the wilderness are dried up, and their course is evil, and their force is not right" (Jer. 23:10).

Daniel, in arguing the ascension of the Antichrist, declared, "Neither shall he regard the God of his fathers, nor the desire of women, nor regard any god: for he shall magnify himself above all. But in his estate shall he honour the God of forces: and a god whom his fathers knew not shall he honour with gold, and silver, and precious stones, and pleasant things" (Dan. 11:38).

Christ contributed, "And from the days of John the Baptist until now the kingdom of heaven suffereth violence, and the violent take it by force"* (Matt. 11:12). While John wrote of the Master, "When Jesus therefore perceived that they would come and take Him by force to make Him a king, He departed again into a mountain Himself alone" (John 6:15).

Paul, a lawyer, in referring to the laws regarding wills, wrote, "For where a testament is, there must also of necessity be the death of the testator. For a testament is of force after men are dead: otherwise it is of no strength at all while the testator liveth" (Heb. 9:16-17).

My favorite Scripture regarding the use of force, however, is essentially a Biblical obituary. Deuteronomy 34:7 documents, "Moses was an hundred and twenty years old when he died: his eye was not dim, nor his natural force abated."

The Hebrew word translated "force" in the verse above is the same Hebrew word as "moist" in, "He [a Nazarite] shall separate himself from wine and strong drink, neither shall he drink any liquor of grapes, nor eat moist grapes, or dried" (Num. 6:3); and "green" in, "And all the trees of the field shall know that I the Lord have brought down the high tree, have exalted the low tree, have dried up the green tree, and have made the dry tree to flourish" (Ezek. 17:24).

Paul perceived, "Though our outward man perish, yet the inward man is renewed day by day" (2 Cor. 4:16). Serving the Lord will keep one's spirit so "fresh" that others will, frankly, be green with envy.

---

*Joseph Thayer's *Greek-English Lexicon* renders the phrase as: "a share in the heavenly kingdom is sought with most ardent zeal and intense exertion."

Chapter Sixty-Five

Blessings Will Chase You Down

There are over five hundred references to "blessing" in the Bible. The Lord told Abraham, "And I will make of thee a great nation, and I will bless thee, and make thy name great; and thou shalt be a blessing: and I will bless them that bless thee, and curse him that curseth thee: and in thee shall all families of the earth be blessed" (Gen. 12:3).

David wrote: "Blessed is the nation whose God is the Lord" (Ps. 33:12); "O taste and see that the Lord is good: blessed is the man that trusteth in Him" (Ibid., 34:8); and, "Blessed is the man that feareth the Lord, that delighteth greatly in His commandments. His seed shall be mighty upon the earth: the generation of the upright shall be blessed. Wealth and riches shall be in his house" (Ibid., 112:1-3).

Solomon said: "Blessings are upon the head of the just" (Prov. 10:6); "The blessing of the Lord, it maketh rich, and He addeth no sorrow with it" (Ibid., 10:22); "By the blessing of the upright the city is exalted" (Ibid., 11:11); "He that saith unto the wicked, 'Thou art righteous;' him shall the people curse, nations shall abhor him: but to them that rebuke him shall be a delight, and a good blessing shall come upon them" (Ibid., 24:24-25); and, "A faithful man shall abound with blessings" (Ibid., 28:20).

Jeremiah joined with,

Blessed is the man that trusteth in the Lord, and whose
hope the Lord is. For he shall be as a tree planted by
the waters, and that spreadeth out her roots by the
river, and shall not see when heat cometh, but her leaf
shall be green; and shall not be careful in the year of
drought, neither shall cease from yielding fruit. (Jer.
17:7-8)

One of the most unique Scriptures regarding blessings is
Deuteronomy 28:2: "And all these blessings shall come on
thee, and overtake thee, if thou shalt hearken unto the voice of
the Lord thy God." In other words, the blessings will *chase you
down!* Then it goes on to list what those blessings are:

Blessed shalt thou be in the city and blessed shalt thou
be in the field. Blessed shall be the fruit of thy body,
and the fruit of thy ground, and the fruit of thy cattle,
the increase of thy kine, and the flocks of thy sheep.
Blessed shall be thy basket and thy store. Blessed shalt
thou be when thou comest in, and blessed shalt thou be
when thou goest out. The Lord shall cause thine enemies that rise up against thee to be smitten before thy
face: they shall come out against the one way, and flee
before thee seven ways. The Lord shall command the
blessing upon thee in thy storehouses, and in all that
thou settest thine hand unto; and He shall bless thee in
the land which the Lord thy God giveth thee. (Deut.
28:3-8)

Some people worry because they think the Lord wants to
"take over" their lives and control them in ways they may not
like. It is more accurate to say that the Lord wants to "overtake" their lives—with blessings!

Chapter Sixty-Six

A Gracious Host

The Hebrew word translated "gracious" in the Old Testament means "to bend or stoop in kindness to an inferior." There are thirty-four references to gracious activity in the Bible, only two of which are mentioned in the New Testament.

The Lord told Moses,

> If thou at all take thy neighbour's raiment to pledge, thou shalt deliver it unto him by that the sun goeth down: for that is his covering only, it is his raiment for his skin: wherein shall he sleep? And it shall come to pass, when he crieth unto Me, that I will hear; for I am gracious. (Exod. 22:26-27)

When Moses asked to see God's glory, He told him, "I will make all My goodness pass before thee, and I will proclaim the name of the Lord before thee; and will be gracious to whom I will be gracious, and will shew mercy on whom I will shew mercy" (Ibid., 33:19).

Moses angrily broke the original tables [sic] of stone, upon which were written the Ten Commandments, after seeing the Israelites worshipping false idols. Later, the Lord told Moses to hew two new tablets out of stone, like the first ones. After doing so, Moses rose early in the morning and went up into Mount Sinai, taking the tables with him (Ibid., 34:4).

It was up on the mountain that the Lord passed before Moses and proclaimed, "The Lord, the Lord God, merciful and gracious, longsuffering, and abundant in goodness and truth, keeping mercy for thousands, forgiving iniquity and transgression and sin" (Ibid., 34:6-7).

On another occasion, the Lord told Moses to instruct Aaron and his sons on how to bless the children of Israel. The Lord told Aaron and his sons to say these words to the people: "The Lord bless thee, and keep thee: the Lord make His face shine upon thee, and be gracious unto thee: the Lord lift up His countenance upon thee, and give thee peace" (Num. 6:24-26).

David directed: "Thou, O Lord, art a God full of compassion, and gracious, longsuffering, and plenteous in mercy and truth" (Ps. 86:15); "Gracious is the Lord, righteous; yea, our God is merciful" (Ibid., 116:5); and, "Remove from me the way of lying: and grant me Thy law graciously" (Ibid., 119:29).

Isaiah, insightful as always, advanced, "Therefore will the Lord wait, that He may be gracious unto you, and therefore will He be exalted, that He may have mercy upon you: for the Lord is a God of judgment: blessed are all they that wait for Him. For the people shall dwell in Zion at Jerusalem: thou shalt weep no more: He will be very gracious unto thee at the voice of thy cry; when He shall hear it, He will answer thee" (Isa. 30:18-19).

Why did Jonah disobey the Lord's order to go to Nineveh and pronounce judgment against it? Was it because Jonah didn't want to condemn anyone or say negative things against the Ninevites? No. Jonah, told us why he really ran away, when he complained to the Lord, "Therefore I fled before unto Tarshish: for I knew that Thou art a gracious God, and merciful, slow to anger, and of great kindness, and repentest thee of the evil" (Jonah 4:2).

Get that! Jonah was "displeased exceedingly" because he knew if he pronounced judgment against Nineveh that God would probably repent and change His mind about destroying the city, leaving Jonah looking like some fool. The Lord had to use a plant to teach Jonah a lesson in compassion—to show him he was "off his gourd."

Once, after Jesus finished quoting a prophetic Scripture regarding His ministry, He closed the book. The Bible says that, "the eyes of all them that were in the synagogue were fastened on Him" (Luke 4:20). Two verses later it says that, "all bare Him witness, and wondered at the gracious words which proceeded out of His mouth" (Ibid., 4:22). The Greek word translated "gracious" in this verse is *charis*, from which is derived the English word: *charisma*.

Christ, the original charismatic, gave a great example of His graciousness when He said, "Behold, I stand at the door, and knock: if any man hear My voice, and open the door, I will come in to him, and will sup with him, and he with Me" (Rev. 3:20).

Yes, God is a gentleman. He won't force His way in where He is not wanted.

Chapter Sixty-Seven

"Such and Such" Things

One evening, King David happened to be walking upon the roof of his palace when he saw a beautiful woman bathing and lusted after her. David then inquired and found out that the woman, Bathsheba, was the wife of one of his soldiers, Uriah. David sent his messengers to bring the woman to him and he committed adultery with her. Afterward, she returned to her own house. When Bathsheba found out she was pregnant, she sent and told David, "I am with child" (2 Sam. 11:5).

David then hatched a diabolical plot. He had his general, Joab, bring Bathsheba's husband, Uriah, from the war. David then told Uriah to go and spend the night with his wife. He wanted others to think Uriah was the father of the child.

Uriah, however, spent the night outside the door of King David's palace, and when David asked him why he did so, Uriah replied, "The ark, and Israel, and Judah, abide in tents; and my lord Joab, and the servants of my lord, are encamped in the open fields; shall I then go into mine own house, to eat and to drink, and to lie with my wife? As thou livest, and as thy soul liveth, I will not do this thing" (Ibid., 11:11).

David thereafter invited Uriah to eat dinner with him and proceeded to get him drunk. Afterwards, Uriah still would not sleep in his own home (Ibid., 11:13). Finally, David wrote a letter to Joab, which he sent by the hand of Uriah! It said: "Set ye Uriah in the forefront of the hottest battle, and retire ye from him, that he may be smitten, and die" (Ibid., 11:14). David had an innocent man murdered!

Approximately nine months later, the Lord sent Nathan the prophet to speak to David. Nathan told him a story about a rich man who had many flocks and a poor man who had only one little ewe lamb. One day a traveller came to call. The rich man, rather than selecting a sheep from his own vast herd, instead killed the poor man's ewe lamb and cooked it for the traveller to eat (Ibid., 12:1-4).

David's anger was aroused and he said to Nathan, "As the Lord liveth, the man that hath done this thing shall surely die: and he shall restore the lamb fourfold, because he did this thing, and because he had no pity" (Ibid., 12:5-6). Nathan then looked David in the eyes and said,

> Thou art the man. Thus saith the Lord God of Israel, I anointed thee king over Israel, and I delivered thee out of the hand of Saul; and I gave thee thy master's house, and thy master's wives unto thy bosom, and gave thee the house of Israel and of Judah; and if that had been too little, I would moreover have given unto thee such and such things. Wherefore hast thou despised the commandment of the Lord, to do evil in His sight? (2 Sam. 12:7-9)

No matter how much the Lord has already blessed us, if we will continue obeying His commandments, there are even more "such and such things" which He is willing to give us, if we will resist temptation to do evil.

Chapter Sixty-Eight

I Love a Mystery

I love mysteries.

Give me: gumshoes with gumption, private eyes and plain-clothesmen, cloak-and-dagger capers, invisible ink and incognito interrogations, smoke-screens and stealth, spies and secret agents, sleuths and shamuses, diplomacy and deception, artifice and autopsies, inspector inquires and investigations, murder mysteries, probes and pryings, armchair analysis, cryptic codes, underground and undercover undertakings, escapades and espionage, schemes and stratagems, flatfoots and fingerprints, feds and felonies, hideouts and hoodlums, detectives and dead ends, sherlocks and shadowings, classified files and confidential folders, intuitive reflection and inductive reasoning, rummaging and ransacking, scrounging and scavenging, whodunits and wiretaps, ferreting facts and friskings, combing and canvassing, hunches and hounds, traces and telltale signs, intelligence and informers, mouthpieces and mugs, decoys and deception, stake-outs and surveillance, unearthing, unmasking and unraveling, culprits and criminology, grilling by guards, clues and cunning, stiffs and skeletons, second-guessings and sniffing scents, tracking trails, looked for leads, stooges and stool-pigeons, thugs and troopers, coppers and convicts, suspects and safe-crackers, crimestoppers and commissioners, warrants and wardens, officers and operatives, tear gas throwings and third degree treatments, bull horns and brutes, thrilling tabloids, sensational scoops.

Christ also loved mysteries. The disciples came and said unto Jesus, "Why speakest thou unto them in parables?" Christ replied "Because it is given unto you to know the mysteries of the kingdom of heaven, but to them it is not given. For whosoever hath, to him shall be given, and he shall have more abundance" (Matt. 13:11-2).

In the book of Revelation, Christ told John, "Write the things which thou hast seen, and the things which are, and the things which shall be hereafter, the mystery of the seven stars which thou sawest in My right hand, and the seven golden candlesticks" (Rev. 1:19-20).

Paul publicized much regarding mysteries:

"For I would not, brethren, that ye should be ignorant of this mystery , lest ye should be wise in your own conceits, that blindness in part is happened to Israel, until the fulness of the Gentiles be come in" (Rom. 11:25); "But we speak the wisdom of God in a mystery, even the hidden wisdom, which God ordained before the world unto our glory" (1 Cor. 2:7); "Let a man so account of us, as of the ministers of Christ, and stewards of the mysteries of God" (Ibid., 4:1);

"Behold, I shew you a mystery, we shall not all sleep, but shall be changed, in a moment, in the twinkling of an eye, at the last trump: for the trumpet shall sound, and the dead shall be raised incorruptible, and we shall be changed" (Ibid., 15:51); "Having made known to us the mystery of His will, according to His good pleasure which He hath purposed in Himself" (Eph. 1:9); "For this cause shall a man leave his father and mother, and shall be joined unto his wife, and they two shall be one flesh. This is a great mystery: but I speak concerning Christ and the church" (Ibid., 5:31-32);

Whereof I am made a minister, according to the dispensation of God which is given to me for you, to fulfil the word of God, even the mystery which hath been hid from ages and from generations, but now is made manifest to His saints: to whom God would make known what is the riches of the glory of the mystery among the Gentiles, which is Christ in you, the hope of glory. (Col. 1:25-27)

"And without controversy great is the mystery of godliness: God was manifest in the flesh, justified in the Spirit, seen of angels, preached unto the Gentiles, believed on in the world, received up into glory" (Ibid., 3:16).

Yet, without love, the understanding of mysteries yields nothing. For Paul wrote: "And though I have the gift of prophecy, and understand all mysteries, and all knowledge, and though I have all faith, so that I could remove mountains, and have not charity [Greek: love], I am nothing" (1 Cor. 13:2); and, "That their hearts might be comforted, being knit together in love, and unto all riches of the full assurance of understanding, to the acknowledgment of the mystery of God, and of the Father, and of Christ" (Col. 2:2).

Chapter Sixty-Nine

A Disciplined Mind

Paul wrote to Timothy, his disciple, "For God hath not given us the spirit of fear; but of power, and of love, and of a sound mind" (2 Tim. 1:7). The Greek word translated "sound," here, is *sophronismos*, meaning "disciplined." Of all the other instances where the word "sound" is used in the New Testament (e.g., *sound* words, *sound* doctrine, *sound* of a trumpet), 2 Timothy 1:7 is the only occasion where that particular Greek word is used.

Paul told Titus, "Teach the young women to be sober, to love their husbands, to love their children, to be discreet, chaste, keepers at home, good, obedient to their own husbands, that the word of God be not blasphemed. Young men likewise exhort to be sober minded" (Titus 2:4-6). The words "sober," "sober-minded," and "discreet," above, all use Greek words that mean either "of *sound mind*" or "*disciplined.*"

When Paul witnessed to Governor Festus about Christ, the ruler remarked with a loud voice, "Paul, thou art beside thyself; much learning it make thee mad" (Acts 26:24). Paul replied, "I am not mad, most noble Festus; but speak forth the words of truth and soberness" (Ibid., 26:25). A similar Greek word, meaning "of sound mind," is again used for soberness.

In Titus 2:2, Paul commanded, "That the aged men be sober (Greek: *abstaining* from wine), grave, temperate, sound (Greek: *healthy*) in faith, in charity, in patience." "Temperate," as used here, comes from a Greek word meaning "safe in mind" or "disciplined."

Paul told Timothy that women, "shall be saved in child-bearing, if they continue in faith and charity and holiness with sobriety" (1 Tim. 2:15). The word "sobriety" here does not have anything to do with a person's level of intoxication, but rather—you guessed it—"a disciplined mind."

Paul told the Christians in Rome, "For I say, through the grace given unto me, to every man that is among you, not to think of himself more highly than he ought to think; but to think soberly" (Rom. 12:3). A Greek word meaning "a disciplined mind" is again used.

Finally, Peter persuaded, "Gird up the loins of your mind, be sober [abstain from wine], and hope to the end for the grace that is to be brought unto you at the revelation of Jesus Christ" (1 Pet. 1:13). A disciplined mind is one that is girded up. Thoughts which are allowed to roam randomly oftentimes produce chaos.

Chapter Seventy

Last One Standing Wins

David wrote: "Some trust in chariots, and some in horses: but we will remember the name of the Lord our God. They are brought down and fallen: but we are risen, and stand upright" (Ps. 20:7-8); "My foot standeth in an even place: in the congregations will I bless the Lord" (Ibid., 26:12); "They forgat God their Saviour, which had done great things in Egypt; therefore He said that He would destroy them, had not Moses His chosen stood before Him in the breach, to turn away His wrath" (Ibid., 106:21, 23);

"Thus they provoked Him to anger with their inventions: and the plague brake in among them. Then stood up Phinehas, and executed judgment: and so the plague was stayed" (Ibid., 106:29-30); and, "I was glad when they said unto me, 'Let us go into the house of the Lord.' Our feet shall stand within thy gates, O Jerusalem" (Ibid., 122:1-2).

Solomon stressed: "The house of the righteous shall stand" (Prov. 12:7); and, "Stand not in an evil thing" (Eccles. 8:3); while Jeremiah joined with, "Shall evil be recompensed for good? For they have digged a pit for my soul. Remember that I stood before Thee to speak good for them, and to turn away Thy wrath from them" (Jer. 18:20).

Christ commented, "Every kingdom divided against itself is brought to desolation; and every city or house divided against itself shall not stand" (Matt. 12:25). Paul taught: "Who art thou that judgest another man's servant? To his own master he standeth or falleth. Yea, he shall be holden up: for God is able to make him stand" (Rom. 14:4); "Wherefore let him that thinketh he standeth take heed lest he fall" (1 Cor. 10:12); "Watch ye, stand fast in the faith, quit you like men, be strong" (Ibid., 16:13);

"Stand fast therefore in the liberty where with Christ hath made us free, and be not entangled again with the yoke of bondage" (Gal. 5:1); "Wherefore take unto you the whole armour of God, that ye may be able to withstand in the evil day, and having done all, to stand. Stand therefore, having your loins girt about with truth" (Eph. 6:13-14); "Stand fast in one spirit, with one mind striving together" (Phil. 1:27); and, "Stand perfect and complete in all the will of God" (Col. 4:12).

Those who are called to perform great tasks or champion noble causes often must go it alone first before others eventually buy in to their visions. It makes sense. Those to whom the dreams were given have a greater passion to see its fulfillment because the inspiration comes from inside themselves.

Paul understood this. In 2 Timothy 4:16-17, he wrote, "At my first answer no man stood with me, but all men forsook me: I pray God that it may not be laid to their charge. Notwithstanding the Lord stood with me, and strengthened me." The Lord will always stand by you, for He said, "I will never leave thee, nor forsake thee" (Heb. 13:5).

Angels also stand by people. Gabriel,* "stood to confirm and to strengthen" King Darius (Dan. 11:1). Paul told the sailors who were transporting him, "there stood by me this night the angel of God, whose I am, and whom I serve, saying, 'Fear not, Paul' " (Acts 27:23).

Christ has stood by multitudes of people throughout the ages. One day He is going to make His last stand. For Job prophesied, "I know that my Redeemer liveth, and that He shall stand at the latter day upon the earth" (Job 19:25).

---

*See Daniel 8:16 and 9:21.

Chapter Seventy-One

Winter of Divine Discontent

After King Saul twice tried to kill David with a javelin,* the young musician got hold of Goliath's sword (which Ahimelech the priest had been safekeeping ever since David killed the giant) and escaped to a cave at Adullam (1 Sam. 22:1).

When David's family members heard where he had gone, they joined him. The Bible also states that, "every one that was in distress, and every one that was in debt, and every one that was discontented, gathered themselves unto him; and he became captain over them: and there were with about four hundred men" (Ibid., 22:2).

Other Bible translations render "distress" in the above verse as: "in straits," "oppressed," "ill-used," "in trouble," or "in difficulties;" and, "discontented," as "embittered," "dissatisfied," "angry," "unsatisfied," "desperate," "disaffected," "bitter of soul," or "had a grievance."

The 400 men who joined up with David, the fugitive, had reached such points of desperation in their lives that almost anything else was better than where they were. When they saw that the Lord was with David in whatever he did, they decided to chance it and take part in a cause greater that anything they had yet experienced.

---

*1 Samuel 18:11 and 19:10.

What military skills did those "discontented" men possess? 1 Chronicles records that they, "were armed with bows, and could use both the right hand and the left in hurling stones and shooting arrows out of a bow" (12:2). Verse eight of the same chapter states: "Of the Gadites there separated themselves unto David into the hold to the wilderness men of might, and men of war fit for the battle, that could handle shield and buckler, whose faces were like the faces of lions, and were as swift as the roes upon the mountains."

David's men once invaded the Geshurites, Gezrites, and the Amalekites and smote them, leaving none alive (1 Sam. 27:8-9). On another occasion, they smote more Amalekites, which had attacked the city where David and his men had been living, and smote them from the twilight even unto the evening of the next day. None escaped, except for four hundred men who fled upon camels (Ibid., 30:17). The sons of Gad, captains of the host who joined David, had before been over other soldiers, varying from groups of one hundred to one thousand (1 Chron. 12:14).

When talented people find themselves in a "3-D condition"—either distressed, in debt, or discontented—they need to seek for divine direction so they will then be put into positions where they can perform even mightier deeds.

Chapter Seventy–Two

The Lone Stranger

There are over 200 references to strangers in the Bible. The Lord told Abraham, "I will give unto thee, and to thy seed after thee, the land wherein thou art a stranger, all the land of Canaan, for an everlasting possession; and I will be their God" (Gen. 17:8).

To escape being apprehended by the Egyptian police, Moses went to dwell in the land of Midian. There he married a woman named Zipporah. She bore him a son, whom Moses named Gershom [Hebrew: *refugee*]; for he said, "I have been a stranger in a strange land" (Exod. 11:22).

Moses recorded a lot on the subject of strangers: "Also thou shalt not oppress a stranger: for ye know the heart of a stranger, seeing ye were strangers in the land of Egypt" (Ibid., 23:9); "Six days thou shalt do thy work, and on the seventh day thou shalt rest: that thine ox and thine ass may rest, and the son of thy handmaid, and the stranger, may be refreshed" (Ibid., 23:12); "And if a stranger sojourn with thee in your land, ye shall not vex him. But the stranger that dwelleth with you shall be unto you as one born among you, and thou shalt love him as thyself; for ye were strangers in the land of Egypt" (Lev. 19:33-34);

"And when ye reap the harvest of your land, thou shalt not make clean riddance of the corners of thy field when thou reapest, neither shalt thou gather any gleaning of thy harvest: thou shalt leave them unto the poor, and to the stranger: I am the Lord your God" (Ibid., 23:22); "Ye shall have one manner of law, as well for the stranger, as for one of your own country: for I am the Lord thy God" (Ibid., 24:22); "The land shall not be sold for ever: for the land is Mine; for ye are strangers and sojourners with Me" (Ibid., 25:23); "And if thy brother be waxen poor, and fallen in decay with thee; then thou shalt relieve him: yea, though he be a stranger, or a sojourner; that he may live with thee" (Ibid., 25:35);

"Ye shall not eat of any thing that dieth of itself: thou shalt give it unto the stranger that is in thy gates, that he may eat it; or thou may sell it unto an alien" (Deut. 14:21);

> At the end of three years thou shalt bring forth all the tithe of thine increase the same year, and shalt lay it up within thy gates: and the Levite, (because he hath no part nor inheritance with thee,) and the stranger, and the fatherless, and the widow, which are within thy gates, shall come, and shall eat and be satisfied; that the Lord thy God may bless thee in all the work of thine hand which thou doest. (Deut. 14:28-29)

"Thou shalt not abhor an Egyptian; because thou wast a stranger in his land" (Ibid., 23:7).

In Solomon's monumental prayer in 1 Kings, he made a special request regarding strangers: "Moreover concerning a stranger, that is not of thy people Israel, but cometh out of a far country for Thy name's sake; (for they shall hear of Thy great name, and of Thy strong hand, and of Thy stretched out arm;) when he shall come and pray toward this house; hear Thou in heaven thy dwelling place, and do according to all that the stranger calleth to thee for: that all people of the earth may know Thy name, to fear Thee" (8:41-43).

Christ commented, "He that entereth in by the door is the Shepherd of the sheep. To Him the porter openeth; and the sheep hear His voice: and he calleth His own sheep by name, and leadeth them out. And when He putteth forth His own sheep, He goeth before them, and the sheep follow Him: for they know His voice. And a stranger will they not follow, but will flee from him: for they know not the voice of strangers" (John 10:2-5).

To the Gentiles, Paul wrote, "Ye were without Christ, being aliens from the commonwealth of Israel, and strangers from the covenants of promise, having no hope, and without God in the world: but now in Christ Jesus ye who sometimes were far off are made nigh by the blood of Christ" (Eph. 2:12-13).

Most of us, at one time or another, have felt like strangers. Job and David experienced this. Job said, "My kinsfolk have failed, and my familiar friends have forgotten me. They that dwell in my house, and my maids, count me for a stranger" (Job 19:14-15). David echoed this feeling saying, "For Thy sake I have borne reproach; shame hath covered my face. I am become a stranger unto my brethren, and an alien unto my mother's children" (Ps. 69:7-8).

Whenever you feel isolated, and say to yourself something like: "Let me alone; for my days are vanity" (Job 7:16); "Let me alone, that I may take comfort a little" (Ibid., 10:20); or, "I watch, and am as a sparrow alone upon the housetop" (Ps. 102:7), you must pray like David did: "Hear my prayer, O Lord, and give ear unto my cry; hold not Thy peace at my tears: for I am a stranger with Thee and a sojourner, as all my fathers were" (Ibid., 39:12). Yes, the Lord is the original "Lone Stranger."

Chapter Seventy–Three

God's Will Is a Delight

While attending church for many years, I feared the will of God. I was afraid that if I gave God my best, He would make me miserable like I'd seen so many Christians. Then, one day I reread a verse in Psalms and my spiritual eyes were suddenly opened. It was the passage where David said, "I delight to do Thy will, O my God" (Ps. 40:8). David, who lived an exciting life as an influential and wealthy world leader, was telling us "God's will is fun!"

Jesus said, "For whosoever shall do the will of My Father which is in heaven, the same is My brother, and sister, and mother" (Matt. 12:50). Undoubtedly Jesus always had his mother's best interests at heart, right? If we do the will of God, we can be just as close to Christ as members of His own earthly family.

Ananias, the first disciple to pray for Paul (Acts 9:17), said to the apostle, "The God of our fathers hath chosen thee, that thou shouldest know His will, and see that Just One, and shouldest hear the voice of His mouth" (Ibid., 22:14).

Paul mentioned much about the will of God: "Be ye transformed by the renewing of your mind, that ye may prove what is that good, and acceptable, and perfect, will of God" (Rom. 12:2); "That I may come unto you with joy by the will of God, and may with you be refreshed" (Ibid., 15:32);

"That ye may stand perfect and complete in all the will of God" (Col. 4:12); "Ye have need of patience, that, after ye have done the will of God, ye might receive the promise" (Heb. 10:36); and,

"Now the God of peace, that brought again from the dead our Lord Jesus, that great Shepherd of the sheep, through the blood of the everlasting covenant, make you perfect in every good work to do His will, working in you that which is well-pleasing in His sight through Jesus Christ" (Ibid., 13:20-21).

James wrote, "Go to now, ye that say, 'Today or tomorrow we will go into such a city, and continue there a year and buy and sell, and get gain': whereas ye know not what shall be on the morrow. For what is your life? It is even a vapour, that appeareth for a little time, and then vanisheth away. For that ye ought to say, 'If the Lord will, we shall live, and do this, or that' " (James 4:13-15).

Luke launched forth with, "For David, after he had served his own generation by the will of God, fell on sleep, and was laid unto his fathers" (Acts 13:36). The perfect will of God is that every Christian serve his own generation to whatever degree possible. When that happens, the Lord will be able to say to that person what He said to David, "I have found David the son of Jesse, a man after Mine own heart, which shall fulfill all My will" (Ibid., 13:22).

Chapter Seventy-Four

Slick Smites

Mosaic law foreshadowed the subject of modern-day compensatory damages when it laid down the payment recoverable by one who had been smitten. Exodus 21:18-19 reveals: "And if men strive together, and one smite another with a stone, or with his fist, and he die not, but keepeth his bed: if he rise again, and walk abroad upon his staff, then shall he that smote him be quit [acquitted]: only he shall pay for the loss of his time, and shall cause him to be thoroughly healed."

When Elisha, the prophet, was terminally ill, Joash, the king of Israel, went to him to be blessed. Elisha told him to take an arrow and shoot it out the window. The king did so. Elisha then told Joash that the arrow would be the Lord's deliverance from Syria. The prophet next said to take the remaining arrows and smite the ground. The king smote the ground only three times. The man of God became angry with the king and said, "Thou shouldest have smitten four or five times; then hadst thou smitten Syria till thou hadst consumed it: whereas now thou shalt smite Syria but thrice" (2 Kings 13:19).

Jesus told His disciples, "And unto him that smiteth thee on the one cheek offer also the other" (Luke 6:29). Later, when the high priest struck Jesus with the palm of his hand because of an answer He had given, the Lord demanded, "If I have spoken evil, bear witness of the evil: but if well, why smitest thou Me?" (John 8:23).

In a prophecy regarding the Messiah, Isaiah issued, "I gave My back to the smiters, and My cheeks to them that plucked off the hair: I hid not My face from shame and spitting" (Isa.

50:6). The prophecy was later fulfilled when Pilate had Jesus scourged (John 19:1).

Matthew reported that no sooner had Jesus breathed His last breath then, "the earth did quake, and the rocks rent; and the graves were opened; and many bodies of the saints which slept arose, and came out of the graves after His resurrection, and went into the holy city, and appeared unto many" (Matt. 27:51-53). Luke, in describing this same event, logged, "And all the people came together to that sight, beholding the things which were done, smote their breasts, and returned" (Luke 23:48). The Greek word used for breasts here is *stethos*, from which we get the English word "*stethos*cope."

When the high priest Ananias commanded one of his men to smite apostle Paul, he, being the legal advocate that he was, fired back, "God shall smite thee, thou whited wall: for sittest thou to judge me after the law, and commandest me to be smitten contrary to the law?" (Acts 23:3). When those who stood by said, "Revilest thou God's high priest?" Paul replied respectfully, "I wise [knew] not, brethren, that he was the high priest: for it is written, 'Thou shalt not speak evil of the ruler of thy people'" (Ibid., 23:5).

When Herod threw Peter into prison to please the unbelieving Jews, Luke recorded that while Peter was sleeping, "The angel of the Lord came upon him, and a light shined in the prison: and he smote Peter on the side, and raised him up, saying, 'Arise up quickly'" (Acts 12:7).

Most of the smiting incidences which have been discussed so far in this chapter have involved evil people as the perpetrators. What should be the response when one is smitten by a *righteous* person? David distinguished this with, "Let the righteous smite me; it shall be a kindness: and let him reprove me; it shall be an excellent oil, which shall not break my head: for yet my prayer also shall be in their calamities" (Ps. 141:5).

Correction, even if sternly administered, from those who are righteous, it will do us good. And, though it may seem like it at the time, it won't kill us. To keep the right attitude, we should also respond in the way that David recommended—pray for those who do the reproving.

Chapter Seventy-Five

Idle Worship

The Lord listed the reasons why the city of Sodom was destroyed. He said, "Behold, this was the iniquity of thy sister Sodom, pride, fulness of bread, and abundance of idleness was in her and in her daughters, neither did she strengthen the hand of the poor and needy. And they were haughty, and committed abomination" (Ezek. 16:49-50). Later in the same book, the Lord said, "And I will send a fire on Magog, and among them that dwell carelessly in the isles" (Ibid., 39:6).

In the book of Isaiah, the Lord told the Chaldeans,

> Therefore hear now this, thou that art given to pleasures, that dwelleth carelessly, that sayest in thine heart, "I am, and none else beside me; I shall not sit as a widow, neither shall I know the loss of children": But these two things shall come to thee in a moment in one day, the loss of children, and widowhood: they shall come upon thee in their perfection for the multitude of thy sorceries, and for the great abundance of thine enchantments. (Isa. 47:8-9)

Earlier, the Lord had said, "Rise up, ye women that are at ease; hear My voice, ye careless daughters" (Ibid., 32:9).

The Lord also told Jeremiah, "Moab hath been at ease from his youth, and he hath settled* on his lees, and hath not

---

*Same Hebrew word as "idleness" in Ezekiel 16:49.

been emptied from vessel to vessel, neither hath he gone into captivity: therefore his taste remained in him, and his scent is not changed" (Jer. 48:11).

The Lord told Zechariah, "I am very sore displeased with the heathen that are at ease: for I was but a little displeased, and they helped forward the affliction" (Zech. 1:15). David discussed this same theme when he wrote, "Our soul is exceedingly filled with the scorning of those that are at ease, and with the contempt of the proud" (Ps. 123:4).

King Lemuel's mother taught her son a prophecy regarding a virtuous woman. Such a one, said she, "looketh well to the ways of her household, and eateth not the bread of idleness" (Prov. 31:27). Whereas Paul, in referring to some younger widows, said, "they learn to be idle, wandering about from house; and not only idle, but tattlers also and busy bodies, speaking things which they ought not. I will therefore that the younger women marry" (1 Tim. 4:13-14).

Jesus Christ, who is always looking out for our welfare, instructed, "Every idle word that men shall speak, they shall give account thereof in the day of judgment. For by thy words thou shalt be justified" (Matt. 12:36). The Greek word used here for "idle" is derived from the negative particle "not" and "*ergo*" ("to work," from which we get our English word *ergo*nomics meaning "inactive" or "unemployed"). Christ wants our words, and not only our lives, to not be idle.

Chapter Seventy-Six

Dissolving Doubts

Doubt—the scourge of saints, the bane of believers, the pest of preachers, the curse of converts—is, surprisingly, not mentioned much in the Bible. There are only a few dozen references to it, all except two of which are in the New Testament.

After Jesus was resurrected, He appeared to the eleven disciples and, "when they saw Him, they worshipped Him: but some doubted" (Matt. 28:17). To reassure them, Jesus said, "All power is given unto Me in heaven and earth" (Ibid., 28:18).

In talking about faith to His disciples, Jesus said,

> For verily I say unto you, that whosoever shall say unto this mountain, "Be thou removed, and be thou cast into the sea"; and shall not doubt in his heart, but shall believe that those things which he saith shall come to pass; he shall have whatsoever he saith. (Mark 11:23)

In the book of Luke, Jesus said,

> And seek not ye what ye shall eat, or what ye shall drink, neither be ye of doubtful mind. For all these things do the nations of the world seek after: and your Father knoweth that ye have need of these things. But rather seek ye the kingdom of God; and all these things shall be added unto you. (Luke 12:29-31)

The word translated "doubtful" in the preceding verse is the Greek word *meteorizo*, "to raise in midair," from which we get our English word "meteor." The Greek word *meteorizo* (figuratively meaning "anxiety") taken in conjunction with the English word "meteor" show that doubtful thoughts are those which anxiously wander about without a firm destination.

After Jesus and His disciples finished eating their last supper together, Jesus became "troubled in His spirit" and testified, "Verily, verily, I say unto you, that one of you shall betray Me" (John 13:21). The disciples then looked at each other, "doubting of whom He spake" (Ibid., 13:22). The Greek word used here for "doubting" means "to have no way out."

On a certain day, as recorded in the book of Acts, Peter went on his housetop to pray at noontime. He became hungry and while others began to make him a lunch, Peter fell into a trance. He saw a vessel, like a great sheet knit at the four corners, descending from heaven. Inside were all manner of animals: wild beasts, creeping things, and fowls of the air. Then a voice uttered, "Rise, Peter; kill and eat" (Acts 10:13).

Peter replied, "Not so, Lord; for I have never eaten any thing that is common or unclean" (Ibid., 10:14). The voice then spoke a second time, "What God hath cleansed, that call not thou common" (Ibid., 10:15). The voice again told Peter to eat the animals,* and then the vessel returned into heaven. While "Peter doubted in himself what this vision which he had should mean" (Ibid. 10:17), three men came to visit him.

What Peter didn't know was that an angel had appeared to Cornelius, a Gentile, and told him to send for Peter, who would show him the way to salvation. While Peter continued thinking on the vision, the Spirit said to him, "Behold, three men seek thee. Arise therefore, and get thee down, and go with them, doubting nothing: for I have sent them" (Ibid., 10:19-20). Peter went, and the rest is history.

Paul published to the Christians in Rome,

> All food is clean, but it is wrong for a man to eat
> anything that causes someone else to stumble. Blessed
> is the man who does not condemn himself by what he

---

*The voice speaks *thrice*, in relation to Peter, the same number of times that Peter denied the Lord (Matt. 26:69-75) and Jesus asked Peter if he loved Him (John 21:15-17).

approves. But the man who has doubts is condemned if he eats, because his eating is not of faith. (Rom. 14:20, 22-23, NIV)

Paul then told Timothy, "I will therefore that men pray everywhere, lifting up holy hands, without wrath and doubting" (1 Tim. 2:8). The Greek word translated "doubting" here is *dialogismos* (by implication, "dispute"), from which we get our English word "dialogue." The same Greek word is translated "doubtful" in: "Him that is weak in the faith receive ye, but not to doubtful disputations" (Rom. 14:1).

The only two references to doubt in the Old Testament are found in the book of Daniel. When king Belshazzar desired the interpretation of writing which mysteriously appeared on a wall, he called on Daniel and said to him, "I have heard of thee, that the spirit of the gods is in thee, and that light and understanding and excellent wisdom is found in thee. And I have heard of thee, that thou canst make interpretations, and dissolve doubts*" (Dan. 5:14, 16).

The Hebrew word translated "dissolve" in the preceding verse literally means "*to set free*." It is the same word translated "loose" in: "Lo, I see four men loose, walking in the midst of the fire, and they have no hurt; and the form of the fourth is like the Son of God" (Ibid., 3:25).

We should walk with the Son of God because He knows how to dissolve doubts.

---

*The second reference to "doubts" is found in verse 12.

Chapter Seventy-Seven

A Way-Out God

The greatness of God is a vast subject. Moses, just before he died, wrote, "There is none like the God of Jeshurun, who rideth upon the heaven in thy help, and in His excellency on the sky" (Deut. 33:26).

David deliberated: "When I consider Thy heavens, the work of Thy fingers, the moon and the stars, which Thou hast ordained; what is man, that Thou art mindful of him? And the son of man, that Thou visitest him?" (Ps. 8:3-4); and, "Great is the Lord, and greatly to be praised; and His greatness is unsearchable" (Ibid., 145:3).

In referring to the omniscience of the Almighty, the Psalmist projected,

> Whither shall I go from thy Spirit? Or whither shall I flee from thy presence? If I ascend up into heaven, thou art there: if I make my bed in hell, behold, thou art there. If I take the wings of the morning, and dwell in the uttermost parts of the sea; even there shall thy hand lead me, and thy right hand hold me. If I say, "Surely the darkness shall cover me," even the night shall be light about me. Yea, the darkness hideth not from thee; but the night shineth as the day: the darkness and the light are both alike to thee. (Ps. 139:7-12)

Isaiah's insight into the dimensionlessness of divinity was very deep. He heralded: "Hast thou not known? Hast thou not heard, that the everlasting God, the Lord, the Creator of the ends of the earth, fainteth not, neither is weary? There is no searching of His understanding" (Isa. 40:28); and, "For thus saith the high and lofty One that inhabiteth eternity, whose name is Holy; I dwell in the high and holy place, with him also that is of a contrite and humble spirit" (Ibid., 57:15).

Paul's ponderings were also profound: "Now unto the King eternal, immortal, invisible, the only wise God, be honour and glory for ever" (1 Tim. 1:17); "Our Lord Jesus Christ: which in His times He shall shew, who is the King of kings, and Lord of Lords; who only hath immortality, dwelling in the light which no man can approach unto; whom no man hath seen, nor can see: to whom be honour and power everlasting" (Ibid., 6:14-16); and, "O the depth of the riches both of the wisdom and knowledge of God! How unsearchable are His judgments, and His ways past finding out!" (Rom. 11:33).

Since God's ways are past finding out, He will always be a source of surprise, a fountain of fascination, a wellspring of wonderment, and a basis of bewilderment.

Chapter Seventy-Eight

The Love Lord

The two most important Scriptures in the Bible contain the phrase, "Thou shalt love." Jesus said, "Thou shalt love the Lord thy God with all thy heart, and with all they soul, and with all thy mind. This is the first and great commandment. And the second is like unto it, Thou shalt love thy neighbour as thyself. On these two commandments hang all the law and the prophets" (Matt. 22:37-40).

The Bible is chock full of Scriptures about God's love for us. Moses memorialized: "Because He loved thy fathers, therefore He chose their seed after them, and brought thee out in His sight with His mighty power of Egypt" (Deut. 4:37);

"The Lord came from Sinai, and rose up from Seir unto them; He shined forth from mount Paran, and He came with ten thousands of saints: from His right hand went a fiery law for them. Yea, He loved the people" (Ibid., 33:2-3); and,

"The Lord did not set His love upon you, nor choose you, because ye were more in number than any people; for ye were the fewest of all people: but because the Lord loved you, and because He would keep the oath which He had sworn unto your fathers" (Ibid., 7:7-8).

Isaiah emphasized the love God has toward His people when he wrote: "Thou hast in love to my soul delivered it from the pit of corruption: for Thou hast cast all my sins behind Thy back" (Isa. 38:17); and, "In all their affliction He was afflicted, and the angel of His presence saved them: in His love and in

His pity He redeemed them; and He bare them, and carried them all the days of old" (Ibid., 63:9).

In the books of Jeremiah and Hosea, the Lord spoke about His great love toward people when He said, "Yea, I have loved thee with an everlasting love: therefore with lovingkindness have I drawn thee" (Jer. 31:3); and, "I will heal their backsliding, I will love them freely" (Hosea 14:4).

The prophet Zephaniah gave some very interesting insight into God's love when he wrote prophetically, "In that day it shall be said to Jerusalem, 'Fear thou not': and to Zion, 'Let not thine hands be slack.' The Lord thy God in the midst of thee is mighty; He will save, He will rejoice over thee with joy; He will rest in His love, He will joy over thee with singing" (Zeph. 3:17).

The Hebrew word for "rest" above literally means "to scratch, i.e., to fabricate." Though some translations of the Bible render the word as "renew," "refresh," or "be silent," a more accurate interpretation would be "to work at." The same Hebrew word is translated "worker" in: "And king Solomon sent and fetched Hiram out of Tyre. He was a widow's son of the tribe of Naphtali, and his father was a man of Tyre, a worker in brass" (1 Kings 7:13-14). To put it another way, the Lord is willing to "work as a craftsman" in His love for us.

In the New Testament there are many verses describing the Lord's love for us:

"For God so loved the world, that He gave His only begotten Son" (John 3:16); "Having loved His own which were in the world, He loved them unto the end" (Ibid., 13:1); "As the Father hath loved Me, so have I loved you: continue ye in My love" (Ibid., 15:9); "The love of God is shed abroad in our hearts by the Holy Ghost" (Rom. 5:5); "God, who is rich in mercy, for His great love wherewith He loved us" (Eph. 2:4).

"Walk in love, as Christ also hath loved us" (Ibid., 5:2); "After that the kindness and love of God our Saviour toward man appeared" (Titus 3:4); "Hereby perceive we the love of God, because He laid down His life for us" (1 John 3:16); "And we have known and believed the love that God hath to us. God is love" (Ibid., 4:16); and, "We love Him, because He first loved us" (Ibid., 4:19).

Chapter Seventy-Nine

Sinless Anger

There are almost 300 references to anger in the Bible, and nearly 200 to wrath. About anger and wrath, Solomon submitted: "Grievous words stir up anger" (Prov. 15:1); "He that is slow to anger appeaseth strife" (Ibid., 15:18); "The discretion of a man deferreth his anger; and it is his glory to pass over a transgression" (Ibid., 19:11); "Be not hasty in thy spirit to be angry; for anger resteth in the bosom of fools" (Eccles. 7:9); "He that is soon angry dealeth foolishly" (Prov. 14:17); "It is better to dwell in the wilderness, than with a contentious angry woman" (Ibid., 21:19); "Make no friendship with an angry man; and with a furious man thou shalt not go: lest thou learn his ways, and get a snare to thy soul" (Ibid., 22:24-25); "An angry man stirreth up strife, and a furious man aboundeth in transgression" (Ibid., 29:22);

"He that is slow to wrath is of great understanding" (Ibid., 14:29); "A soft answer turneth away wrath" (Ibid., 15:1); "A man of great wrath shall suffer punishment: for if thou deliver him, yet thou must do it again" (Ibid., 19:19); "Proud and haughty scorner is his name, who dealeth in proud wrath" (Ibid., 21:24); "Scornful men bring a city into a snare: but wise men turn away wrath" (Ibid., 29:8); and, "Surely the churning of milk bringeth forth butter, and the wringing of the nose bringeth forth blood: so the forcing of wrath bringeth forth strife" (Ibid., 30:33).

James, the brother of Jesus, wrote, "Wherefore my beloved brethren, let every man be swift to hear, slow to speak, slow to wrath" (James 1:19). Paul cautioned, "Fathers, provoke not your children to anger, lest they be discouraged" (Col. 3:21).

Paul then revealed this paradoxical precept: "Be ye angry, and sin not: let not the sun go down upon your wrath" (Eph, 4:26). That is to say, it *is* possible to be angry *without* sinning. The key is not to let the anger smolder overnight. Don't let the sun set without first getting rid of your anger.

Chapter Eighty

From Murderer to Mentor

Moses once murdered an innocent man in cold blood.

The stepson of a Pharaoh, Moses "was learned in all the wisdom of the Egyptians, and was mighty in words and in deeds" (Acts 7:22). One day, when Moses was "grown,"* he "went out unto his brethren, and looked on their burdens: and he spied an Egyptian smiting an Hebrew, one of his brethren" (Exod. 2:11). Moses, "looked this way and that way, and when he saw that there was no man, he slew the Egyptian, and hid him in the sand" (Ibid., 2:12).

To convict someone of a criminal offence under Anglo-American law, the prosecution must prove the following elements: (1) *Actus Reus*–a guilty act by defendant; (2) *Mens Rea*–a guilty mind of defendant at time of act; (3) Concurrence–physical act and mental state existed at same time; and, (4) Harmful Result and Causation–result was both *factually* and *proximately* caused by defendant's act. Murder is defined as the unlawful killing of a human being (*actus reus*) with malice aforethought (*mens rea*). Intent to kill is one of the states of mind that constitutes malice aforethought.

---

*Acts 7:2 states that Moses was 40-years-old at the time of this incident.

Voluntary manslaughter, like murder, is an intentional killing, but committed in the "heat of passion" (i.e., adequate provocation). For the provocation to be legally adequate, there are four requirements that must be met: (1) the provocation must arouse sudden and intense passion in the mind of an ordinary person such as to cause him to lose control; (2) defendant must have in fact been provoked; (3) there must not have been a reasonable "cooling off" period; and (4) defendant in fact didn't cool off between the provocation and the killing.

Adequate provocation is generally recognized if the defendant is being subjected to a serious battery or threat of deadly force. In Moses' case, the Hebrew was being smitten by the Egyptian. Therefore, Moses could not claim the defense of voluntary manslaughter.

Today Moses would be guilty of murder, unless he could have claimed "defense of others" as an excuse. To do so, he would've had to reasonably believe that the Hebrew he assisted had the legal right to use deadly force against the Egyptian. Since the Hebrews were slaves of the Egyptians of the time, they likely had no, or very few, rights. Thus, Moses did not have the right to use deadly force under the circumstances.

Regardless of any defense, the danger to the Hebrew was already past (the Bible didn't say that the Hebrew servant was killed, but only that he was "oppressed" by the Egyptian [Acts 7:24]). Moses' act would therefore be one of unlawful retaliation (under modern law) and not in defense of others.

Under modern law, a deliberate and premeditated killing is first degree murder and carries a stiffer punishment than second degree murder. "Deliberate" means that the defendant intended to kill in a cool and dispassionate manner. "Premeditated" means that the defendant actually reflected on the idea of killing, even if only for a short period of time. Since Moses "looked this way and that way" and then waited until "he saw that there was no man" around before he slew the Egyptian, Moses was thus guilty of Murder One under the laws in force today.

Rules similar to our modern laws were evidently in effect in Egypt at that time because Moses hid the body in the sand

and then fled when the matter became known. Hiding a body is direct evidence of guilt, while fleeing the scene of a crime is circumstantial evidence of *mens rea.* Solomon, a judge himself, issued a similar opinion of law when he wrote, "he that hasteth with his feet sinneth" (Prov. 19:2).

Even though Moses murdered a man and never officially paid for the crime (although living in the desert for forty years may have been God's measure of punishment for the offense), he was still mightily used by God. In fact, Moses not only became a mentor for several million Israelites during his own lifetime, he also became a role model to almost a hundred generations after his death.

Toward the end of His ministry, the Lord took Peter, John, and James up into a mountain to pray. As Jesus prayed, "His countenance was altered, and His raiment was white and glistering" (Luke 9:29). The Bible then states that: "There talked with Him two men, who were Moses and Elias. Who appeared in glory, and spake of His decease which He should accomplish of Jerusalem" (Luke 9:30-31). Thus when even Jesus Himself wanted to talk to someone about important matters, He went to Moses.

Chapter Eighty-One

Right-handed Pleasure

The word pleasure is mentioned sixty-eight times in the Bible. One of the first instances is in Deuteronomy 23:24. It is a rather startling Scripture, considering our current laws regarding trespass to property, for it states, "When thou comest into thy neighbor's vineyard, then thou mayest eat grapes thy fill at thine own pleasure; but thou shalt not put any in the vessel."

Other pleasure precepts are: "I know also, my God, that Thou triest the heart, and hast pleasure in uprightness" (1 Chron. 29:17); "Let them shout for joy, and be glad, that favour my righteous cause: yea, let them say continually, 'Let the Lord be magnified, which hath pleasure in the prosperity of His servant'" (Ps. 35:27); "The works of the Lord are great, sought out of all them that have pleasure therein" (Ibid., 111:2);

"For the Lord taketh pleasure in His people" (Ibid., 149:4); "Fear not, little flock; for it is your Father's good pleasure to give you the kingdom" (Luke 12:32); and "Wherefore also we pray always for you, that our God would count you worthy of this calling, and fulfil all the good pleasure of His goodness, and the work of faith with power" (2 Thess. 1:11).

Too much pleasure, or the wrong kind, is harmful according to Solomon. He said, "He that loveth pleasure shall be a poor man: he that loveth wine and oil shall not be rich" (Prov. 21:17). Also, the pleasures of sin are temporary. Paul wrote, "By faith Moses, when he was come to years, refused to be called the son of Pharaoh's daughter; choosing rather to suffer affliction with the people of God, than to enjoy the pleasures of sin for a season" (Heb. 11:24-25).

Man may try, but he can't imitate or improve upon the kind of pleasure that God offers, David decided. He said, "They shall be abundantly satisfied with the fatness of Thy house; and thou shalt make them drink of the river of Thy pleasures" (Ps. 36:8).

David declared, "Thou wilt shew me the path of life: in Thy presence is fulness of joy; at Thy right hand there are pleasures for evermore" (Ibid., 16:11). The Hebrew word for pleasures, as used in this verse, is mentioned on only one other occasion—the first time it occurs in the Bible. Genesis 18:10 states that the Lord told Sarah, who was 90-years-old at the time, that she was going to have a son, "according to the time of life" (i.e., in nine months). Sarah then laughed within herself and said, "After I am waxed old shall I have pleasure, my lord being old also?" The Hebrew word here for "pleasure" (and in Ps. 16:11) is *eden*, the name of the garden in the book of Genesis.

Chapter Eighty-Two

Something You Can Always Ask For—And Get

The Bible talks a lot about "asking." After Jacob wrestled with an angel until the break of day, Jacob said to the heavenly emissary, "Tell me, I pray thee, thy name." The angel answered, "Wherefore is it that thou dost ask after my name?" The angel then "blessed him there" (Gen. 32:29).

When Manoah, the father-to-be of Samson, asked an angel his name so when his sayings came to pass Manoah could honor him, the angel of the Lord answered, "Why askest thou thus after my name, seeing it is secret?" (Judg. 13:18).

When the time had come that the Lord was going to take up Elijah into heaven by a whirlwind, Elijah said unto Elisha, "Ask what I shall do for thee, before I be taken away from thee." Elisha replied, "I pray thee, let a double portion of thy spirit be upon me" (2 Kings 2:9).

When the Lord said to king Ahaz, "Ask thee a sign of the Lord thy God; ask it either in the depth, or in the height above," Ahaz answered, "I will not ask, neither will I tempt the Lord" (Isa. 7:12). The Lord responded, "Is it a small thing for you to weary men, but will ye weary My God also?" (Ibid., 7:13).

The Lord impelled Isaiah to write, "Thus saith the Lord, the Holy One of Israel, and His Maker, 'Ask Me of things to come concerning My sons, and concerning the work of My hands command ye Me'" (Isa. 45:11).

The Lord told Jeremiah: "Thus saith the Lord, Stand ye in the ways, and see and ask for the old paths, where is the good way, and walk therein, and ye shall find rest for your souls" (Jer. 6:16); and, "They shall ask the way to Zion with their faces thitherward, saying, 'Come, and let us join ourselves to the Lord in a perpetual covenant that shall not be forgotten'" (Ibid., 50:5).

The Lord then told Zechariah, "Ask ye of the Lord rain in the time of the latter rain; so the Lord shall make bright clouds, and give them showers of rain, to every one grass in the field" (Zech. 10:1).

In the New Testament, these Scriptures can be found regarding the subject of asking: "Ask, and it shall be given you; seek, and ye shall find; knock, and it shall be opened unto you" (Matt. 7:7); "Hitherto have ye asked nothing in My name: ask, and ye shall receive, that your joy may be full" (John 16:24); "And all things, whatsoever ye shall ask in prayer, believing, ye shall receive" (Matt. 21:22); "If ye abide in Me, and My words abide in you, ye shall ask what ye will, and it shall be done unto you" (John 15:7); "Now unto Him that is able to do exceeding abundantly above all that we ask or think, according to the power that worketh in us, unto Him be glory in the church by Christ Jesus throughout all ages, world without end" (Eph. 3:20-21); "And this is the confidence that we have in Him that, if we ask any thing according to His will, He heareth us" (1 John 5:14).

In all our asking, there is one thing that God *will always give us,* and He'll never put us down for asking! James 1:5 boldly states: "If any of you lack wisdom, let him ask of God, that giveth to all men liberally, and upbraideth not*;

---

*Other Bible translations render "upbraideth not" as: without scolding; ungrudgingly; without reproach; without faultfinding; without refusing; without reserve; without resentment; will not be condescending; gives graciously; won't correct for asking; enjoys giving it.

and it shall be given him." The next verse does go on to say, "But let him ask in faith, nothing wavering. For he that wavereth is like a wave of the sea driven with the wind and tossed."

The famous scientist, Isaac Newton, believed his concepts and ideas were given to him by the Holy Spirit. There is no end to the wisdom that will be imparted to us, if we will but ask!

Chapter Eighty-Three

Thou Shalt Not Give to the Rich

The Bible relates some interesting things regarding the rich, starting with David: "Be not thou afraid when one is made rich, when the glory of his house is increased; for when he dieth he shall carry nothing away" (Ps. 49:16-17). The Hebrew word for "afraid" in this verse is the same word translated as "reverence" in: "God is greatly to be feared in the assembly of the saints, and to be had in reverence of all them that are about Him" (Ibid., 89:7). In other words, we are not to reverence the rich. David also said, "If riches increase, set not your heart upon them" (Ibid., 62:10).

Solomon, who was very wealthy, stated: "Strong men retain riches" (Prov. 11:16); "He that trusteth in his riches shall fall" (Ibid., 11:28); "Wealth gotten by vanity shall be diminished" (Ibid., 13:11); "The rich hath many friends" (Ibid., 14:20); "The poor useth entreaties; but the rich answereth roughly" (Ibid., 18:23); "The rich and the poor meet together: the Lord is the maker of them all" (Ibid., 22:2); and, "He that maketh haste to be rich shall not be innocent" (Ibid., 28:20).

Jeremiah added: "Thus saith the Lord, Let not the wise man glory in his wisdom, neither let the mighty man glory in his might, let not the rich man glory in his riches" (Jer. 9:23); and, "As the partridge sitteth on eggs, and hatcheth them not; so he that getteth riches, and not by right, shall leave them in the midst of his days, and at his end shall be a fool" (Ibid., 17:11).

Paul wrote, "Charge them who are rich in this world, that they be not high-minded, nor trust in uncertain riches, but in the living God, who giveth us richly all things to enjoy" (1 Tim. 6:17).

The most unusual verse regarding the rich, however, is found in Proverbs. Solomon, the richest man to ever live,* cautioned, "He that oppresseth the poor to increase his riches, and he that giveth to the rich, shall surely come to want"** (Prov. 22:16).

---

*2 Chronicles 1:12 records what the Lord promised Solomon: "I will give thee riches, and wealth, and honour, such as none of the kings have had that have been before thee, neither shall there any after thee have the like."

**Hebrew: *deficiency*

Chapter Eighty-Four

Peace Officers

There are over 425 references to peace in the Bible. Almost every time the word is mentioned in the Old Testament, the Hebrew word *Shalom* is used. It means "to be safe in mind or body." The word "peace" is used in many different contexts. When the Pharaoh needed his dream interpreted, Joseph said to him, "It is not in me: God shall give Pharaoh an answer of peace" (Gen. 41:16).

Moses said: "The Lord shall fight for you, and ye shall hold your peace" (Exod. 14:14); "An altar of earth thou shalt make unto Me, and shalt sacrifice thereon thy burnt offerings, and thy peace offerings, thy sheep, and thine oxen: in all places where I record My name I will come unto thee, and I will bless thee" (Ibid., 20:24); "I will give peace in the land, and ye shall lie down, and none shall make you afraid: and I will rid evil beasts out of the land, neither shall the sword go through your land" (Lev. 26:6); and, "When thou comest nigh unto a city to fight against it, then proclaim peace unto it. And it shall be, if it make thee answer of peace, and open unto thee, then it shall be that all the people that is found therein shall be tributaries unto thee, and they shall serve thee" (Deut. 20:10-11).

David dictated: "Do good; seek peace, and pursue it" (Ps. 34:14); "The meek shall inherit the earth; and delight themselves in the abundance of peace" (Ibid., 37:11); "Mark the perfect man, and behold the upright: for the end of that man is peace" (Ibid., 37:37); "The mountains shall bring peace to the people, and the little hills, by righteousness" (Ibid., 72:3);

"Mercy and truth are met together; righteousness and peace have kissed each other" (Ibid., 85:10); "Great peace have they which love Thy law: and nothing shall offend them" (Ibid., 119:165); and, "Pray for the peace of Jerusalem: they shall prosper that love thee" (Ibid., 122:6).

Solomon wrote: "Happy is the man that findeth wisdom, and the man that getteth understanding. Her ways are ways of pleasantness, and all her paths are peace" (Prov. 3:13, 17); and, "To the counsellors of peace is joy" (Ibid., 12:20). And Isaiah revealed: "Thou wilt keep him in perfect peace, whose mind is stayed on Thee: because he trusteth in Thee" (Isa. 26:3); "The work of righteousness shall be peace" (Ibid., 32:17); and, "O that thou hadst hearkened to My commandments! Then had thy peace been as a river" (Ibid., 48:18).

Paul continued: "Glory, honour, and peace, to every man that worketh good" (Rom. 2:10); "To be spiritually minded is life and peace" (Ibid., 8:6); "For the kingdom of God is not meat and drink; but righteousness, and peace, and joy in the Holy Ghost" (Ibid., 14:17); "Endeavouring to keep the unity of the Spirit in the bond of peace" (Eph. 4:3); and, "For it pleased the Father that in Him should all fulness dwell; and, having made peace through the blood of His cross, by Him to reconcile all things unto Himself" (Col. 1:19-20).

The final authority on the subject of peace, of course, is Jesus Christ. Verses regarding the Lord as the source of peace are: "He was wounded for our transgressions, He was bruised for our iniquities: the chastisement of our peace was upon Him; and with His stripes we are healed" (Isa. 53:5); "To give light to them that sit in darkness and in the shadow of death, to guide our feet in the way of peace" (Luke 1:79); "These things I have spoken unto you, that in Me ye might have peace" (John 16:33); and, "The peace of God, which passeth all understanding, shall keep your hearts and minds through Christ Jesus" (Phil. 4:7).

A prophecy by Isaiah regarding the birth of Christ is, however, the controlling Scripture regarding the subject of peace. It states, "For unto us a Child is born, unto us a Son is given: and the government shall be upon His shoulder: and His name

shall be called Wonderful, Counsellor, The Mighty God, The
everlasting Father, The Prince of Peace. Of the increase of His
government and peace there shall be no end" (Isa. 9:6-7).

Chapter Eighty-Five

Thou Shalt Not Be Discouraged

Discouragement is mentioned seven times in the Bible. In six of the instances, a different Hebrew word is used for the same English translation.

The first time the word "discourage" is used is in Numbers, the twenty-first chapter. There it is recorded that the children of Israel, "journeyed from mount Hor by the way of the Red Sea, to compass the land of Edom: and the soul of the people was much discouraged because of the way" (Num. 21:4). The Hebrew word used there means "to dock off; curtail."

The next two times the word "discourage" is used occur in the thirty-second chapter of Numbers; Moses said to the children of Gad and to the children of Reuben,

> Shall your brethren go to war, and shall ye sit here? And wherefore discourage ye the heart of the children of Israel from going over into the land which the Lord hath given them? Thus did your fathers, when I sent them from Kadesh-barnea to see the land. For when they went up unto the land, they discouraged the heart of the children of Israel, that they should not go into the land which the Lord had given them. (Num. 32:6-9)

The Hebrew word used in the two instances above means

"to dissuade."

The next two times the word "discourage" is used occur in the first chapter of Deuteronomy. Moses told the people, "Behold, the Lord thy God hath set the land before time: go up and possess it, as the Lord God of thy fathers hath said unto thee; 'Fear not, neither be discouraged' " (Deut. 1:21). The word "discouraged" here is translated, "broken down."

Six verses later, Moses said to the people,

> Ye murmured in your tents, and said, "Because the Lord hated us, He hath brought us forth out of the land of Egypt, to deliver us into the hand of the Amorites, to destroy us." Whither shall we go up? Our brethren have discouraged our heart, saying, "The people is greater and taller than we." (Deut. 1:27)

The word "discouraged" here means "make faint."

Paul wrote in the book of Colossians, "Fathers, provoke not your children to anger, lest they be discouraged" (Col. 3:21). The Greek word used here for "discouraged" means "spiritless." In Isaiah 42:4 is a prophecy of Jesus Christ which foretells that, "He shall not fail nor be discouraged, till He have set judgment in the earth." The Hebrew word used for "discouraged" here means "cracked in pieces."

Jesus is our example in all things. Though Christ experienced grief (Isa. 53:3), sorrow and heaviness (Matt. 26:37), and weariness (John 4:6), they never caused Him to "crack in pieces." Just as Christ had to fulfill the prophecy in Isaiah, and He is our pattern to follow, so we must also fulfill the same commandment–to not be discouraged.

Chapter Eighty-Six

The Sliding Scale of Grace

Grace is mentioned 161 times in the Bible. The Old Testament word for "grace" comes from a Hebrew root meaning "to bend or stoop in kindness to another." The New Testament word for "grace" comes from a Greek root meaning "to be cheerful."

Because Noah was a just man, perfect in his lifetime, and walked with God, he, "found grace in the eyes of the Lord" (Gen. 6:8). Moses said to God, "I pray Thee, if I have found grace in Thy sight, shew me now Thy way, that I may know Thee, that I may find grace in Thy sight: and consider that this nation is Thy people." God replied, "My presence shall go with thee, and I will give thee rest" (Exod. 33:13-14).

Gideon said to the heavenly visitor who had just told him he was to deliver Israel from the hand of the Midianites, "If now I have found grace in thy sight, then shew me a sign that thou talkest with me" (Judg. 6:17). When the angel touched the dressed goat and unleavened cakes with the end of his staff, fire arose out of the rock and consumed the items.

Solomon supported: "Keep sound wisdom and discretion: so shall they be life unto thy soul, and grace to thy neck" (Prov. 3:21-22); "He scorneth the scorners: but He giveth grace to the lowly" (Ibid. 3:34); and, "Wisdom is the principal thing; therefore get wisdom . . . she shall give to thine head an ornament of grace: a crown of glory shall she deliver to thee" (Ibid., 4:7, 9).

Luke wrote, "I commend you to God, and to the word of His grace, which is able to build you up, and to give you an inheritance among all them which are sanctified" (Acts 20:32). And John joined with, "And of His fulness have all we received, and grace for grace. For the law was given by Moses, but grace and truth came by Jesus Christ" (John 1:16-17).

Paul wrote: "For all have sinned, and come short of the glory of God; being justified freely by His grace through the redemption that is in Christ Jesus" (Rom. 3:23-24); "For all things are for your sakes, that the abundant grace might through the thanksgiving of many redound to the glory of God" (2 Cor. 4:15); "For ye know the grace of our Lord Jesus Christ, that, though He was rich, yet for your sakes He became poor, that ye through His poverty might be rich" (Ibid., 8:9); "God is able to make all grace abound toward you; that ye, always having all sufficiency in all things, may abound to every good work" (Ibid., 9:8);

"In whom we have redemption though His blood, the forgiveness of sins, according to the richness of His grace" (Eph. 1:7); "That in the ages to come He might shew the exceeding riches of His grace in His kindness toward us through Christ Jesus. For by grace are ye saved through faith; and that not of yourselves: it is the gift of God" (Ibid., 2:7-8); and, "Now our Lord Jesus Christ Himself, and God, even our Father, which hath loved us, and hath given us everlasting consolation and good hope through grace, comfort your hearts, and stablish you in every good word and work" (2 Thess. 2:16-17).

The most intriguing verse regarding grace is found in the book of Romans: "Moreover the law entered that the offense might abound. But where sin abounded, grace did much more abound" (Rom. 5:20). In other words, the worse the surrounding or predicament, the greater grace that will be given.

Ephesians 4:7 corroborates this concept, with, "But unto every one of you is given grace according to the measure of the gift of Christ." Further substantiating this (and the only time Jesus talked about grace) is 2 Corinthians 12:9, which states, "My grace is sufficient for thee."

Chapter Eighty-Seven

Folks with Yokes

Jehovah told the Jews, "I am the Lord your God, which brought you forth out of the land of Egypt, that ye should not be their bondmen; and I have broken the bands of your yoke, and made you go upright" (Lev. 26:13).

Again, the Almighty said, "Thus saith the Lord God of hosts, 'O My people that dwellest in Zion, be not afraid of the Assyrian . . . it shall come to pass in that day, that his burden shall be taken away from off thy shoulder, and his yoke from off thy neck, and the yoke shall be destroyed because of the anointing' " (Isa. 10:27).

Mentioning the missing of meals, the Lord said,

> Is it such a fast that I have chosen? A day for a man to afflict his soul? Is it to bow down his head as a bulrush, and to spread sackcloth and ashes under him? Wilt thou call this a fast, and an acceptable day to the Lord? Is not this the fast that I have chosen? To loose the bands of wickedness, to undo the heavy burdens, and to let the oppressed go free, and that ye break every yoke? (Isa. 58:5-6)

To Israel and Judah the Lord prophesied,

> Alas! For that day is great, so that none is like it: it is even the time of Jacob's trouble; but he shall be saved out of it. For it shall come to pass in that day, saith the Lord of hosts, that I will break his yoke from off thy neck, and will burst thy bonds, and strangers shall no

more serve themselves of him: But they shall serve the
Lord their God, and David their king, whom I will
raise up unto them"* (Jer. 30:7-8).

In another prophecy regarding the coming of the Messiah,
the Lord said,

> And I will set up one Shepherd over them, and He
> shall feed them, even My servant David; He shall feed
> them, and He shall be their Shepherd. And the tree of
> the field shall yield her fruit, and the earth shall yield
> her increase, and they shall be safe in their land, and
> shall know that I am the Lord, when I have broken the
> bands of their yoke. (Ezek. 34:23, 27)

In the book of Hosea, the Lord lamented, "I taught
Ephraim also to go, taking them by their arms; but they knew
not that I healed them. I drew them with cords of a man, with
bands of love: and I was to them as they that take off the yoke
on their jaws, and I laid meat unto them" (11:3-4).

In the New Testament, the Lord encouraged, "Take My
yoke upon you, and learn of Me; for I am meek and lowly in
heart: and ye shall find rest unto your souls. For My yoke is
easy and My burden is light" (Matt. 11:29-30). The Greek word
translated "easy" in this verse means "employed i.e., useful."

A yoke is a wooden frame used to harness together two
beasts of burden, e.g. oxen. If two oxen each similar in age,
size, and weight can pull by themselves 4,000 pounds, you
would think that together they would be able to pull 8,000
pounds, right? Wrong. They can pull *10,000* pounds. Why?
Because of the scientific principle called "synergism." It holds
that the combined action is greater in total effect than the sum
of their efforts.

You and Christ can accomplish much together. The yoke
Christ offers is useful to your life and will lead you to optimum

---

*This is a prophecy of the coming Messiah.

employment opportunities. But regarding certain kinds of yokes Paul precautioned: "Stand fast therefore in the liberty wherewith Christ hath made us free, and be not entangled again with the yoke of bondage" (Gal. 5:1); and, "Be ye not unequally yoked together with unbelievers" (2 Cor. 6:14).

Chapter Eighty-Eight

A Sowing Machine

As befitting the agricultural society that existed during its authorship, the Bible makes many references to sowing and reaping. The Lord told Moses: "And six years thou shalt sow thy land, and shalt gather in the fruits thereof: but the seventh year thou shalt let it rest and lie still; that the poor of thy people may eat: and what they leave the beasts of the field shall eat. In like manner thou shalt deal with thy vineyard, and with thy oliveyard" (Exod. 23:10);

> If ye walk in My statutes, and keep My commandments, and do them; then I will give you rain in due season, and the land shall yield her increase, and the trees of the field shall yield their fruit. And your threshing shall reach unto the vintage, and the vintage shall reach unto the sowing time; and ye shall eat your bread to the full, and dwell in your land safely. (Lev. 26:3-5)

"Thou shalt not sow thy vineyard with divers seeds: lest the fruit of thy seed which thou hast sown, and the fruit of thy vineyard, be defiled. Thou shalt not plow with an ox and an ass together" (Deut. 22:9-10).

David, who was born on a farm, talked much about sowing in his writings. He held forth: "Light is sown for the righteous, and gladness for the upright in heart" (Ps. 97:11); "They that sow in tears shall reap in joy. He that goeth forth and weepeth, bearing precious seed, shall doubtless come again with rejoicing, bringing his sheaves with him" (Ibid., 126:5-6); and, "He turneth the wilderness into a standing water, and dry ground into watersprings. And there He maketh the hungry to dwell, that they may prepare a city for habitation; and sow the fields, and plant vineyards, which may yield fruits of increase. He blesseth them also, so that they are multiplied greatly" (Ibid., 107:35-38).

When Solomon wrote, "He that observeth the wind shall not sow; and he that regardeth the clouds shall not reap" (Eccles. 11:4), he was basically saying that those who wait for the perfect conditions never accomplish anything. In referring to the wisdom of pursuing different opportunities throughout one's life, the sage said, "In the morning sow thy seed, and in the evening withhold not thine hand: for thou knowest not whether shall prosper, either this or that, or whether they both shall be alike good" (Ibid., 11:6).

Isaiah insisted: "Blessed are ye that sow beside all waters, that send forth thither the feet of the ox and the ass" (Isa. 32:20); and, "For as the earth bringeth forth her bud, and as the garden causeth the things that are sown in it to spring forth; so the Lord God will cause righteousness and praise to spring forth before all nations" (Ibid., 61:11).

In a prophecy regarding the Gentiles becoming saved, the Lord told Hosea,

> And it shall come to pass in that day, I will hear, saith the Lord, I will hear the heavens, and they shall hear the earth; and the earth shall hear the corn, and the wine, and the oil; and they shall hear Jezreel. And I will sow her unto me in the earth; and I will have mercy upon her that had not obtained mercy; and I will say to them which were not My people, "Thou art My people"; and they shall say, "Thou art my God." (Hosea 2:21-23)

Later in the same chapter, the Lord said, "Sow to yourselves in righteousness, reap in mercy; break up your fallow ground: for it is time to seek the Lord, till He come and rain righteousness upon you" (Ibid., 10:12).

The word of the Lord came to Jeremiah and said, "Go and

cry in the ears of Jerusalem, saying, 'Thus saith the Lord; I
remember thee, the kindness of thy youth, the love of thine
espousals, when thou wentest after Me in the wilderness, in a
land that was not sown'" (Jer. 2:2). And the Lord educated
Ezekiel, "For, behold, I am for you, and I will turn unto you,
and ye shall be tilled and sown: And I multiply men upon you,
all the house of Israel, even all of it: and the cities shall be
inhabited, and the wastes shall be builded" (Ezek. 36:9-10).

Jesus joined with,

> And he that reapeth receiveth wages, and gathereth
> fruit unto life eternal: that both he that soweth and he
> that reapeth may rejoice together. And herein is that
> saying true, "One soweth, and another reapeth." I sent
> you to reap that whereon ye bestowed no labour: other
> men laboured, and ye are entered into their labours.
> (John 4:36-38)

And Jesus' brother added, "And the fruit of righteousness
is sown in peace of them that make peace" (James 3:18).

Paul wrote: "He which soweth bountifully shall reap also
bountifully" (2 Cor. 9:6); "Whatsoever a man soweth, that shall
he also reap" (Ibid., 9:7); and, "He that soweth to the Spirit
shall of the Spirit reap life everlasting" (Gal. 6:8). And he
heartened all Christians with, "Let us not be weary in well
doing: for in due season we shall reap, if we faint not" (Ibid.,
6:9).

Chapter Eighty-Nine

Solitary Confinement

The word "lonely" does not appear in the *King James Bible.* The first time the word "alone" appears is Genesis 2:18, where the Lord (in referring to Adam) told the angels, "It is not good that the man should be alone; I will make him an help meet for him."

David wrote, "God setteth the solitary in families" (Ps. 68:6). The Hebrew word for "solitary" here is *yachiyd,* which is translated "forsaken" in: "I have been young, and now am old; yet have I not seen the righteous forsaken, nor his seed begging for bread" (Ibid., 37:25); and "only" in: "I will pour upon the house of David, and upon the inhabitants of Jerusalem, the spirit of grace and of supplications: and they shall look upon Me whom they have pierced, and they shall mourn for Him, as one mourneth for His only son" (Zech. 12:10).

David also wrote:

> They wandered in the wilderness in a solitary way; they found no city to dwell in. Hungry and thirsty, their soul fainted in them. Then they cried unto the Lord in their trouble, and He delivered them out of their distresses. And He led them forth by the right way, that they might go to a city of habitation. Oh that men would praise the Lord for His goodness, and for His wonderful works to the children of men! (Ps. 107:4-8)

The Hebrew word for "solitary" in the preceding verse is *yeshiymown,* which is translated "desert" in: "Behold, I will do a new thing; now it shall spring forth; shall ye not know it? I will even make a way in the wilderness, and rivers in the desert" (Isa. 43:19); and "wilderness" in: "The Lord's portion is His people; Jacob is the lot of His inheritance. He found him in a desert land, and in the waste howling wilderness; He led him about, He instructed him, He kept him as the apple of his eye" (Deut. 32:9-10).

The Lord must have alluded to the individual nature of a person's call to greatness when He told the people of Israel, "Look unto to Abraham your father, and unto Sarah that bare you: for I called him alone, and blessed him, and increased him" (Isa. 51:2).

There are many times when a busy person needs to sequester himself from the bustle of daily business for a designated interval. Matthew said of Jesus: "When He had sent the multitudes away, He went up into a mountain apart to pray: and when the evening was come, He was there alone" (Matt. 14:23). Mark also wrote about Jesus on another occasion, "In the morning, rising up a great while before day, He went out, and departed into a solitary place, and there prayed" (Mark 1:35).

Let us now refer to the quote in the first paragraph of this chapter: "It is not good that the man should be alone." At the time the Lord made that statement, Eve had not been created. Since being the sole human being on earth was the only reality Adam knew, he couldn't have understood loneliness because he had not even experienced human companionship at that time. Why did the Lord say what He did? Because it was not good that God be alone.

Chapter Ninety

The Privilege to Bless Others

Most of the over 500 references to blessings in the Bible deal with God blessing His people. In this chapter we will discuss people blessing others.

In Genesis 12:3, God told Abram,* "I will bless them that bless thee; and in thee shall all families of the earth be blessed." After Abram rescued his nephew, Lot, from being kidnapped, Melchizedek, king of Salem, met him and said, "Blessed be Abram of the most high God, possessor of heaven and earth" (Gen. 14:19).

Here are some more people who blessed others:

1. Isaac—"By faith Isaac blessed Jacob and Esau concerning things to come" (Heb. 11:20);
2. Jacob—"Jacob blessed Pharaoh" (Gen. 47:7); "All these are the twelve tribes of Israel: and this is it that their father [Jacob] spake unto them, and blessed them; every one according to his blessing he blessed them" (Ibid., 49:28);
3. Laban—"Early in the morning Laban rose up, and kissed his sons and his daughters, and blessed them" (Gen. 31:55);

---

*This was before God changed his name to Abraham (Gen. 17:5).

4. Moses and Aaron–"Moses and Aaron went into the tabernacle of the congregation, and came out, and blessed the people: and the glory of the Lord appeared unto all the people" (Lev. 9:23);

5. Priests–"The priests the sons of Levi shall come near; for them the Lord thy God hath chosen to minister unto Him, and to bless in the name of the Lord" (Deut. 21:5);

6. Joshua–"When Joshua sent them away also unto their tents, then he blessed them, and he spake unto them, saying, 'Return with much riches unto your tents, and with very much cattle, with silver, and with gold, and with brass, and with iron, and with very much raiment' " (Josh. 22:7-8);

7. Employees of Boaz–"Behold, Boaz came from Bethlehem, and said unto the reapers, 'The Lord be with you.' And they answered him, 'The Lord bless thee' " (Ruth 2:4);

8. Eli–"Eli blessed Elkanah and his wife, and said, 'The Lord give thee seed of this woman for the loan which is lent to the Lord' " (1 Sam. 2:20);

9. Samuel–"As soon as ye be come into the city, ye shall straightway find him [Samuel], before he go up to the high place to eat: for the people will not eat until he come, because he doth bless the sacrifice" (1 Sam. 9:13);

10. David–"When David had made an end of offering the burnt offerings and the peace offerings, he blessed the people in the name of the Lord" (1 Chron. 16:2);

11. Solomon–"The king turned his face about, and blessed all the congregation of Israel" (1 Kings 8:14);

12. Solomon's citizens–"On the eighth day he [Solomon] sent the people away: and they blessed the king, and went unto their tents joyful and glad of heart for all the goodness that the Lord had done" (1 Kings 8:66);

13. Nehemiah's citizens–"The people blessed all the men, that willingly offered themselves to dwell at Jerusalem" (Neh. 11:2).

Jesus Christ knew the power of blessing, for He took children up in His arms, "put His hands upon them, and blessed them" (Mark 10:16). On another occasion Jesus said, "Bless them that curse you, and pray for them which despitefully use you" (Luke 6:28).

Paul, likewise, promoted: "Bless them which persecute you: bless, and curse not" (Rom. 12:14); and, "being reviled, we bless" (1 Cor. 4:12). If we are commanded to bless those who don't like us, how much more should we bless those who *do*!

Can blessings be passed down to succeeding descendants? The answer is an unqualified "Yes." When Jacob blessed his son Joseph, he said, "The blessings of your father [on you] are greater than the blessings of my forefathers [Abraham and Isaac on me] and are as lasting as the bounties of the eternal hills" (Gen. 49:26, *Amplified Bible*).

When you bless another, however, it must be done at a suitable time and in a proper manner. For Solomon admonished, "He that blesseth his friend with a loud voice, rising early in the morning, it shall be counted a curse to him" (Prov. 27:14).

Chapter Ninety-One

Hospitality Is
Next to Heaven

When three strangers (incognito angels) came to call, Abraham had their feet washed, meal cakes made, a calf dressed, and brought butter and milk to give them (Gen. 18:4-8). When two angels, also in the form of men, visited Lot in the city of Sodom, he made them "a feast" (Ibid., 19:2).

An angel, disguised as a man of God (Judg. 13:6), showed up one day at the field of Manoah and his wife. He told them they would have a son whom they were to call Samson. Manoah then gave orders to have a young goat made ready. And, added Job, "The stranger did not lodge in the street: but I opened my doors to the traveller" (Job 31:22).

Zephaniah wrote, "Hold thy peace at the presence of the Lord God: for the day of the Lord is at hand: for the Lord hath prepared a sacrifice, He hath bid His guests" (Zeph. 1:7). Christ later likened the kingdom of heaven to a king who made a marriage for his son. The ruler sent his servants to call those who had been invited to the wedding and they all made excuses as to why they couldn't come. The king then told his servants to go into the highways and gather together as many people as they could find so the wedding would be "furnished with guests" (Matt. 22:10).

When Jesus passed through Jericho, Zacchaeus, the chief of the publicans, wanted to see him. Because the tax collector was short of stature and couldn't see over the crowd of people, he climbed up into a sycamore tree to get a better view. Christ saw Zacchaeus and asked to come to his house. When the other publicans saw what had happened, they murmured against Jesus, saying, "that He was gone to be guest with a man that is a sinner" (Luke 19:7).

Paul prompted: (1) The church at Rome to be, "distributing to the necessity of saints; given to hospitality" (Rom. 12:3); (2) Timothy that, "a bishop then must be blameless, the husband of one wife, vigilant, sober, of good behaviour, given to hospitality" (1 Tim. 3:2); (3) Titus that, "a bishop must be blameless, as the steward of God; not selfwilled, not soon angry, not given to wine, no striker, not given to filthy lucre; but a lover of hospitality" (Titus 1:7-8).

Peter added, "Use hospitality one to another without grudging" (1 Pet. 4:9). And one shouldn't begrudge being hospitable because James said, "Grudge not one against another, brethren, lest ye be condemned: behold, the Judge standeth before the door" (James 5:9).

The word "forgetful" is mentioned only two times in the Bible. The second time the word is used* is in Hebrews, the thirteenth chapter: "Let brotherly love continue. Be not forgetful to entertain strangers: for thereby some have entertained angels unawares" (Heb. 13:1-2). The Greek word for "entertain," which appears before the word "strangers," is the same Greek word that's translated "hospitality" in the verses listed in the third and fourth paragraphs above. Clearly, the impact of hospitality could reach heavenly proportions.

---

*The first time is Hebrews 13:2.

Chapter Ninety-Two

Ms. Wisdom

In the book of Proverbs, there are many verses that portray wisdom as feminine:

> Wisdom crieth without; she uttereth her voice in the streets; she crieth in the chief place of concourse, in the opening of the gates: in the city she uttereth her words, saying, "How long, ye simple ones will ye love simplicity? And the scorners delight in their scorning, and fools hate knowledge? Turn you at my reproof: behold, I will pour out my spirit unto you, I will make known my words unto you." (Prov. 1:20-23)

> My son if thou wilt receive my words, and hide my commandments with thee; so that thou incline thine ear unto wisdom, and apply thine heart to understanding; yea, if thou criest after knowledge, and liftest up thy voice for understanding; if thou seekest her as silver, and searchest for her as for hid treasures; then shalt thou understand the fear of the Lord, and find the knowledge of God. (Ibid. 2:1-5)

> Happy is the man that findeth wisdom, and the man that getteth understanding. For the merchandise of it is better than the merchandise of silver, and the gain thereof than fine gold. She is more precious than rubies: and all the things thou canst desire are not to be compared to her. Length of days is in her right hand; and in her left hand riches and honour. Her ways are

ways of pleasantness, and all her paths are peace. She is a tree of life to them that lay hold upon her: and happy is every one that retaineth her. (Ibid. 3:13-18)

Get wisdom, get understanding: forget it not; neither decline from the words of my mouth. Forsake her not, and she shall preserve thee: love her, and she shall keep thee. Exalt her, and she shall promote thee: she shall bring thee to honour, when thou dost embrace her. She shall give to thine head an ornament of grace: a crown of glory shall she deliver to thee. (Ibid. 4:5-6, 8-9)

Doth not wisdom cry? And understanding put forth her voice? She crieth at the gates, at the entry of the city, at the coming in at the doors. "Unto you, O men, I call; and my voice is to the sons of man. O ye simple, understand wisdom: and, ye fools, be ye of an understanding heart. Hear; for I will speak of excellent things; and the opening of my lips shall be right things." (Ibid. 8:1, 3-6)

Wisdom hath builded her house, she hath hewn out her seven pillars: she hath sent forth her maidens: she crieth upon the highest places of the city, "Whoso is simple, let him turn in hither": as for him that wanteth understanding, she saith to him, "Come, eat of my bread, and drink of the wine which I have mingled. Forsake the foolish, and live; and go in the way of understanding." (Ibid. 9:1, 3-6)

In the last chapter of Proverbs are words of King Lemuel from "the prophecy that his mother taught him" (Ibid., 31:1). The king recorded, "Who can find a virtuous woman? For her price is far above rubies ... she openeth her mouth with wisdom" (Ibid., 31:10, 26). God gives virtuous women special wisdom. Men should embrace the wealth of insight they possess. If a wife is wiser than her husband, he should not feel threatened. He shows how smart *he* was by marrying her!

Chapter Ninety-Three

Your Spirit–
A Mark of Excellence

David wrote: "Blessed is the man unto whom the Lord imputeth not iniquity, and in whose spirit there is no guile" (Ps. 32:2); "The Lord is nigh unto them that are of a broken heart; and saveth such as be of a contrite spirit" (Ibid., 34:18); and, "Create in me a clean heart, O God; and renew a right spirit within me" (Ibid., 51:10).

Solomon specified: "A talebearer revealeth secrets: but he that is of a faithful spirit concealeth the matter" (Prov. 11:13); "Better it is to be of an humble spirit with the lowly, than to divide the spoil with the proud" (Ibid., 16:19); "He that is slow to anger is better than the mighty; and he that ruleth his spirit than he that taketh a city" (Ibid., 16:32); "He that hath no rule over his own spirit is like a city that is broken down and without walls" (Ibid., 25:28); and, "Better is the end of a thing than the beginning thereof: and the patient in spirit is better than the proud in spirit" (Eccles. 7:8).

The Lord told the prophet Ezekiel, "I will give them one heart, and I will put a new spirit within you; and I will take the stony heart out of their flesh, and will give them an heart of flesh" (Ezek. 11:19); while Paul wrote, "Brethren, if a man be overtaken in a fault, ye which are spiritual, restore such an one in the spirit of meekness" (Gal. 6:1); and Peter petitioned wives to have, "the ornament of a meek and quiet spirit, which is in the sight of God of great price" (1 Pet. 3:4).

Regarding an *excellent* spirit, Solomon said, "He that hath knowledge spareth his words: and a man of understanding is of an excellent spirit" (Prov. 17:27). The Hebrew word used here for "excellent" comes from a word which means "to *chill*" (i.e., be cool, calm, and collected).

The Bible says that Daniel, "was preferred above the presidents and princes, because an excellent spirit was in him" (Dan. 6:3). The Hebrew word used for "excellent" here means "preeminent." Because Daniel had such an excellent spirit King Darius, "thought to set him over the whole realm" (Ibid.); King Nebuchadnezzar, "made Daniel a great man, and gave him many great gifts, and made him ruler over the whole province of Babylon, and chief of the governors over all the wise men of Babylon" (Ibid., 2:48); King Belteshazzar, "clothed Daniel with scarlet, and put a chain of gold about this neck, and made a proclamation concerning him, that he should be the third ruler in the kingdom" (Ibid., 5:29); and, "Daniel prospered in the reign of Darius, and in the reign of Cyrus the Persian" (Ibid., 6:28).

Do you want people in high positions to bless you? Have an excellent spirit.

Chapter Ninety-Four

"The Poor Man's Wisdom Is Despised"

The Bible talks a lot about the poor. There are over 210 verses dealing with the subject, such as:

> And when ye reap the harvest of your land, thou shalt not wholly reap the corners of thy field, neither shall thou gather the gleanings of thy harvest. And thou shalt not glean thy vineyard, neither shalt thou gather every grape of thy vineyard; thou shalt leave them for the poor and stranger: I am the Lord your God. (Lev. 19:9-10)

"Blessed is he that considereth the poor: the Lord will deliver him in the time of trouble" (Ps. 41:1); "He that oppresseth the poor reproacheth his Maker: but he that honoureth Him hath mercy on the poor" (Prov. 14:31).

Some of the Biblical reasons for poverty are: "He that loveth pleasure shall be a poor man: he that loveth wine and oil shall not be rich" (Prov. 21:17); "The poor heareth not rebuke" (Ibid., 13:8); and, "Much food is in the tillage of the poor: but there is that is destroyed for want of judgment" (Ibid., 13:23).

Two Scriptures in particular show how the poor are discriminated against: "The poor is hated even of his own neighbor" (Ibid., Prov. 14:21); and, "All the brethren of the poor do hate him: how much more do his friends go far from him? He pursueth them with words, yet they are wanting to him" (Ibid.,

19:7).

Is there hope for the poor? Absolutely. The Bible emphatically states: "The needy shall not always be forgotten: the expectation of the poor shall not perish forever" (Ps. 9:18); "Thou, O God, hast prepared of Thy goodness for the poor" (Ibid., 68:10); "For the Lord heareth the poor, and despiseth not His prisoners" (Ibid., 69:33); "He shall judge the poor of the people, He shall save the children of the needy, and shall break in pieces the oppressor" (Ibid., 72:4); and, "Blessed be ye poor: for yours is the kingdom of God" (Luke 6:20).

I feel the most important attribute the poor can possess is found in the book of James: "Hearken, my beloved brethren, hath not God chosen the poor of this world rich in faith, and heirs of the kingdom which He hath promised to them that love Him?" (James 2:5).

A poor person, with faith, can accomplish much. Jesus said, "If ye have faith as a grain of mustard seed, ye shall say unto this mountain, 'Remove hence to yonder place'; and it shall remove; and nothing shall be impossible to you" (Matt. 17:20). With faith one can believe: "It is He that giveth the power to get wealth" (Deut. 8:18); and that, "He raiseth up the poor out of the dust, and lifteth the needy out of the dunghill; that He may set him with princes" (Ps. 113:7-8).

Moses wrote that, "the poor shall never cease out of the land" (Deut. 15: 11), and Christ corroborated with, "the poor always ye have with you" (John 12:8). But God is well aware of the problem of poverty according to Solomon, who wrote, "If thou seest the oppression of the poor, and violent perverting of judgment and justice in a province, marvel not at the matter: for he that is higher than the highest regardeth; and there be higher than they" (Eccles. 5:8).

Solomon told this story:

> There was once a small city with only a few people in it. And a powerful king came against it, surrounded it and built huge siegeworks against it. Now there lived in that city a man poor but wise, and he saved the city by his wisdom. But nobody remembered that poor man.

So I said, "Wisdom is better than strength," but the
poor man's wisdom is despised, and his words are no
longer heeded. (Eccles. 9:14-16, NIV)

One reason that the Lord wants His people to prosper is
so that their wisdom, which He has given them, will be listened to.

Chapter Ninety-Five

Time Redemption

Time is mentioned over 600 times in the Bible. There are over sixteen Greek words translated "time," including: *epi* (from which we get the English word "*epi*logue"); *chronos* (English word: "*chron*ology"); *archaios* (English word: "*archae*ology"); *hora* (English word: "hour"); and *genea* (English word: "*genea*logy").

Selected Scriptures dealing with the subject of time include: "Is any thing too hard for the Lord? At the time appointed I will return unto thee, according to the time of life, and Sarah shall have a son" (Gen. 18:14); "A wise man's heart discerneth both time and judgment" (Eccles. 8:5); "Thus saith the Lord, in an acceptable time have I heard thee, and in a day of salvation have I helped thee" (Isa. 49:8);

"Ask ye of the Lord rain in the time of the latter rain; so the Lord shall make bright clouds, and give them showers of rain, to every one grass in the field" (Zech. 10:1); "For when we were yet without strength, in due time Christ died for the ungodly" (Rom. 5:6); and, "Judge nothing before the time" (1 Cor. 4:5).

Solomon set forth the most exhaustive continuous exposition concerning time:

> To every thing there is a season, and a time to every purpose under the heaven: a time to be born, and a time to die; a time to plant, and a time to pluck up that which is planted; a time to kill, and a time to heal; a time to break down, and a time to build up; a time to

weep, and a time to laugh; A time to mourn, and a time
to dance; a time to cast away stones, and a time to
gather stones together; a time to embrace, and a time to
refrain from embracing; a time to get, and a time to
lose; a time to keep, and a time to cast away; a time to
rend, and a time to sew; a time to keep silence, and a
time to speak; a time to love, and a time to hate; a time
of war, and a time of peace. (Eccles. 3:1-8)

Paul wrote: "See then that ye walk circumspectly, not as
fools, but as wise, redeeming the time, because the days are
evil" (Eph. 5:15-16); and, "Walk in wisdom toward them that
are without, redeeming the time" (Col. 4:5).

The Greek word for "redeem" in the above two verses
means "to buy up." It is the same Greek word used in: "God
sent forth His Son, made of a woman, made under the law, to
redeem them that were under the law, that we might receive
the adoption of sons" (Gal. 4:4-5). We should use our time as
effectively as possible in order to "buy up" every opportunity.

Chapter Ninety-Six

Daily Downloading of Benefits

All companies offer their own versions of individual benefits packages to employees. The Lord is no different, only His benefits are second to none. David said, "Bless the Lord, O my soul, and forget not all His benefits" (Ps. 103:2). Then he went on to list what they are:

1. Who forgiveth all thine iniquities;
2. Who healeth all thy diseases;
3. Who redeemeth thy life from destruction;
4. Who crowneth thee with lovingkindness and tender mercies;
5. Who satisfieth thy mouth with good things; so that thy youth is renewed like the eagle's. (Ps. 103:2-5)

The Lord continually renders benefits to us. David detailed, "Blessed be the Lord, who daily loadeth us with benefits, even the God of our salvation" (Ps. 68:19). When the Lord keeps us from sickness, harm, wrongdoing, etc., He is also bestowing upon us benefits, though we may not be aware of it at the time.

The Lord's benefits inure to whole nations, as well as to individuals. God told Jeremiah,

> At what instant I shall speak concerning a nation, and concerning a kingdom, to pluck up and to pull down,

and to destroy it; if that nation, against whom I have pronounced, turn from their evil, I will repent of the evil that I thought to do unto them. And at what instant I shall speak concerning a nation, and concerning a kingdom, to build and to plant it; if it do evil in My sight, that it obey not My voice, then I will repent of the good, wherewith I said I would benefit them. (Jer. 18:7-10)

Paul, referring to the master-servant undertaking (principles which can also apply to the employer-employee relationships of today), handed down:

Let as many servants as are under the yoke count their own masters worthy of all honour, that the name of God and His doctrine be not blasphemed. And they that have believing masters, let them not despise them, because they are brethren; but rather do them service, because they are faithful and beloved, partakers of the benefit.

The Greek word that is translated "benefit" in the above verse only, is the identical Greek word as "benefactors" in:

The kings of the Gentiles exercise lordship over them; and they that exercise authority upon them are called benefactors. But ye shall not be so: but he that is greatest among you, let him be as the younger; and he that is chief, as he that doth serve. (Luke 22:25-26)

Paul, who loved to personally benefit others, was willing to do so to individuals on more than one occasion. He wrote to the church at Corinth, "I was minded to come unto you before, that ye might have a second benefit" (2 Cor. 1:15).

David, who was mightily benefited by the Lord, wanted to show his appreciation to the Lord. This is how he did it. He said, "What shall I render unto the Lord for all His benefits toward me? I will take the cup of salvation, and call upon the name of the Lord. I will pay my vows unto the Lord now in the presence of all His people" (Ps. 116:12-14).

Chapter Ninety-Seven

How to Get Your Heart's Desires

Everyone has desires—both spoken and secret; confessed and concealed; divulged and disguised; heralded and hidden. David wrote, "Lord, all my desire is before Thee; and my groaning is not hid from Thee" (Ps. 38:9). Since desires come from the heart we all must share similar desires because David decreed that the Lord: "looketh upon all the inhabitants of the earth. He fashioneth their hearts alike" (Ibid., 33:14-15).

Solomon stated: "Hope deferred maketh the heart sick: but when the desire cometh, it is a tree of life" (Prov. 13:12); and, "The desire accomplished is sweet to the soul" (Ibid., 13:19). Unfulfilled longings, though heart-rending, keep a person sympathetic and benevolent towards others. That's why Solomon said, "The desire of a man is his kindness" (Ibid., 19:22).

I believe there are at least three distinct ways to have the desires of the heart accomplished:

1. Righteousness—"The desire of the righteous shall be granted" (Prov. 10:24).
2. Belief—"What things soever ye desire, when ye pray, believe that ye receive them, and ye shall have them" (Mark 11:24).
3. Delight in the Lord—"Delight thyself also in the Lord; and He shall give thee the desires of thine heart" (Ps. 37:4).

Referring to the last point, am I telling you that merry-making with the Master, festivity with the Father, gaiety with God, joviality with Jesus, etc., can lead to desires being fulfilled? Yes, you can have your cake and eat it, too!

David described some more benefits that accrue to those who exhibit much delight in the Lord: "Blessed is the man that feareth the Lord that delighteth greatly in His commandments. His seed shall be mighty upon the earth: the generation of the upright shall be blessed. Wealth and riches shall be in his house: and his righteousness endureth for ever" (Ps. 112:1-3).

Chapter Ninety-Eight

Beware of Dogs

The word "cat" is not mentioned in the Bible (although there is archaeological evidence of domestic felines in ancient Egypt), but much is said about dogs. The first reference to dogs is just before the original Passover. The Lord said He was going the kill the firstborn of Egypt, from the Pharaoh's family to the firstborn of beasts (Exod. 11:5).

The Lord said the cry of the people would be great and, "against any of the children of Israel shall not a dog move his tongue, against man or beast: that ye may know how that the Lord doth put a difference between the Egyptians and Israel" (Exod. 11:7).

On Mount Sinai the Lord told Moses: "And ye shall be holy men unto Me: neither shall ye eat any flesh that is torn of beasts in the field; ye shall cast it to the dogs" (Ibid., 22:31); and later He said, "Thou shalt not bring the hire of a whore, or the price of a dog, into the house of the Lord thy God for any vow: for even both these are abomination unto the Lord thy God" (Deut. 23:18).

When the Lord chose Gideon to deliver Israel from bondage by the Midianites, thirty-two thousand soldiers joined with him. The Lord told Gideon that it was too many, as they might take the credit for the victory. God had Gideon tell the men who were "fearful and afraid" to return (Judges 7:3). Twenty-two thousand soldiers left. The Lord thought that ten thousand was still too large a number. He told Gideon to take the men down to the water and He would try them there.

Nine-thousand seven-hundred men knelt beside the water and drank with both hands. Each remaining man put only one hand to his mouth and lapped, "of the water with his tongue; as a dog lappeth" (Ibid., 7:5). Those three hundred men were the ones the Lord chose to go with Gideon to win the battle.

Job, during his time of testing, longed for the months past when God had preserved him. He reminiscenced: "Unto me men gave ear, and waited, and kept silence at my counsel. After my words they spake not again; and my speech dropped upon them" (Job 29:21-22). Then Job, commenting on the situation, stated, "But now they that are younger than I have me in derision, whose fathers I would have disdained to have set with the dogs of my flock" (Ibid., 30:1).

Goliath, when he saw David had come out to fight him with only a staff, said, "Am I a dog, that thou comest to me with staves?" (1 Sam. 17:43). The Philistine then proceeded to curse David by his gods. Later David, while fleeing from Saul, said, "After whom is the king of Israel come out? After whom dost thou pursue? After a dead dog, after a flea" (Ibid., 24:14).

David delved some more into the subject of dogs in Psalms: "But be not thou far from me, O Lord: O my strength, haste Thee to help me. Deliver my soul from the sword; my darling from the power of the dog" (Ps. 22:19-20); and, "They return at evening: they make a noise like a dog, and go round about the city. Behold, they belch out with their mouth: swords are in their lips: 'For who,' say they, 'doth hear?' But Thou, O Lord, shalt laugh at them; Thou shalt have all the heathen in derision" (Ps. 59:6-8).

Solomon, too, mentioned dogs: "As a dog returneth to his vomit, so a fool returneth to his folly" (Prov. 26:11); "He that passeth by, and meddleth with strife belonging not to him, is like one that taketh a dog by the ears" (Ibid., 26:17); and, "For to him that is joined to all the living there is hope: for a living dog is better than a dead lion" (Ibid., 9:4).

Christ connected canines to the contemptuous when He said, "Give not that which is holy unto the dogs" (Matt. 7:6). Later, He told a parable about a rich man and a beggar named

Lazarus. Christ commented that the beggar was so poor that, "the dogs came and licked his sores" (Luke 16:21).

The last book of the Bible mentions dogs. John wrote, "For without [the holy city, New Jerusalem] are dogs, and sorcerers" (Rev. 22:15). But I think it's fitting to end this chapter with a quote from which is taken a phrase that has withstood to the present day: "Beware of dogs, beware of evil works, beware of the concision" (Phil. 3:2).

Chapter Ninety–Nine

Think Your Way to Greatness

The Bible says much about how thinking affects a person's actions. Solomon wrote: "The thoughts of the righteous are right" (Prov. 12:5); "Commit thy works unto the Lord, and thy thoughts shall be established" (Ibid., 16:3); "The thoughts of the diligent tend only to plenteousness; but of every one that is hasty only to want" (Ibid., 21:5); and, "Eat thou not the bread of him that hath an evil eye, neither desire thou his dainty meats: for as he thinketh in his heart, so is he" (Ibid., 23:6-7).

The Gospels tell us: "Think not that I am come to destroy the law, or the prophets: I am not come to destroy, but to fulfil" (Matt. 5:17); "When ye pray, use not vain repetitions, as the heathen do: for they think that they shall be heard for their much speaking" (Ibid., 6:7); and, "Search the Scriptures; for in them ye think ye have eternal life" (John 5:39).

Paul, a man of great intellect, penned: "For I say, through the grace given unto me, to every man that is among you, not to think of himself more highly than he ought to think" (Rom. 12:3); "Let every man be fully persuaded in his own mind" (Ibid., 14:5); "That ye might learn in us not to think of men above that which is written, that no one of you be puffed up for one against another" (1 Cor. 4:6);

"And if any man think that he knoweth any thing, he knoweth nothing yet as he ought to know" (Ibid., 8:2); "Charity [love] . . . Is not easily provoked, thinketh no evil" (Ibid., 13:5); "When I was a child, I spake as a child, I understood as a child, I thought as a child: but when I became a man, I put away childish things" (Ibid., 13:11); "For if a man think himself to be something, when he is nothing, he deceiveth himself" (Gal. 6:3); and, "Be renewed in the spirit of your mind" (Eph. 4:23).

Regarding any request for wisdom, James admonished, "Ask in faith, nothing wavering. For he that wavereth is like a wave of the sea driven with the wind and tossed. For let not that man think that he shall receive any thing of the Lord" (James 1:6-7).

Peter posed, "Beloved, think it not strange concerning the fiery trial which is to try you, as though some strange thing happened unto you: but rejoice, inasmuch as ye are partakers of Christ's sufferings; that, when His glory shall be revealed, ye may be glad also with exceeding joy" (1 Pet. 4:12-13).

Paul, true to course, condensed all the thought concepts into one verse: "Finally, brethren, whatsoever things are true, whatsoever things are honest, whatsoever things are just, whatsoever things are pure, whatsoever things are lovely, whatsoever things are of good report; if there be any virtue, and if there be any praise, think on these things" (Phil. 4:8).

Don't Forget to Say, "Thank You"

It is a universal desire to receive some measure of appreciation after giving a gift to someone, even if it's just a simple, "Thank you."

Jesus Christ understood this. One day, as He entered a village, ten lepers* met Him. Standing afar off, they cried out, "Jesus, Master, have mercy on us" (Luke 17:12). Jesus simply told them to go show themselves to the priests. As the ten men left to do so, they were miraculously cleansed! One of them, a Samaritan, when he saw he was healed, turned around and thanked God. Jesus then asked, "Were there not ten cleansed? But where are the nine? There are not found that returned to give glory to God, save this stranger" (Ibid., 17:18).

King David, himself a musician, wrote more about the giving of thanks than any other Old Testament author. His musicians did, "prophesy with harps" and did "give thanks and praise to the Lord" (1 Chron. 25:1,3).

David also declared: "Thou hast delivered me from the violent man. Therefore I will give thanks unto Thee, O Lord,

---

*Leprosy is often called "Hansen's Disease" today because it was a Norwegian physician, G. Armauer Hansen, who, in 1874, discovered the germ that causes the disease.

among the heathen" (2 Sam. 22:29-30); "I will praise the name of God with a song, and will magnify Him with thanksgiving" (Ps. 69:30); "Unto Thee, O God, do we give thanks, unto Thee do we give thanks: for that Thy name is near Thy wondrous works declare" (Ibid., 75:1); and, "O give thanks unto the Lord; for He is good: for His mercy endures for ever" (Ibid., 106:1).

The Lord assured Isaiah that, "the Lord shall comfort Zion: He will comfort all her waste places; and He will make her wilderness like Eden, and her desert like the garden of the Lord; joy and gladness shall be found therein, thanksgiving, and the voice of melody" (Isa. 51:3).

When king Nebuchadnezzar woke up from the nightmare, he commanded his magicians, astrologers, and sorcerers to interpret it. When they asked the king to first *tell* them the dream, the king told them he couldn't remember it, and if they didn't correctly describe the dream so he could recall it, he would cut them in pieces. Daniel, who also stood to lose his life, went to his friends and asked them to pray.

When God revealed the dream and its interpretation to Daniel, he declared, "I thank Thee, and praise Thee, O Thou God of my fathers, who hast given me wisdom and might, and hast made known unto me now what we desired of Thee: for Thou hast now made known unto us the king's matter" (Dan. 2:23).

No sooner had Jonah finished the words, "I will sacrifice unto Thee with the voice of thanksgiving; I will pay that I have vowed. Salvation is of the Lord,"* than the Bible states that, "The Lord spake unto the fish, and it vomited out Jonah upon the dry land" (Ibid., 2:10). Clearly thanksgiving caused the whale not to "stomach" Jonah any longer.

Jesus said, "Father, I thank Thee that Thou hast heard Me. And I knew that Thou hearest Me always: but because of

---

*Jonah 2:9

the people which stand by I said it, that they may believe that Thou hast sent Me" (John 11:41-42). Right after He said those words, Jesus proceeded to raise Lazarus from the dead.

Paul, while with a boatload full of 276 distressed sailors, "took bread, and gave thanks to God in presence of them all" (Acts 27:35). Paul wasn't ashamed to pray for his meal, even in front of a crowd of people. Paul also passed on: "And whatsoever ye do in word or deed, do all in the name of the Lord Jesus Christ, giving thanks to God and the Father by Him" (Col. 3:17);

"In* everything give thanks: for this is the will of God in Christ Jesus concerning you" (1 Thess. 5:18); and,

> Exhort therefore, that, first of all, supplications, prayers, intercessions and giving of thanks, be made for all men; for kings, and for all that are in authority; that we may lead a quiet life in all godliness and honesty. For this is good and acceptable in the sight of God our Saviour. (1 Tim. 2:1-3)

Yes, we should give *thanks* for "kings, and for all that are in authority" because God wants us to.

---

*Note that it says "in" everything, and not necessarily "for" everything.

Faith: The Final Frontier

There are twenty-eight references to faith in the Old Testament.* Compare this to 298 times the word is mentioned in the New Testament** (i.e., over ten times as often); we see that faith was a favorite subject of Christ and His disciples.

The Hebrew word translated as "faith" in the Old Testament means "firmly established"; while the Greek word for "faith" in the New Testament means "persuaded." The Scripture most well known in the Old Testament is, "The just shall live by his faith" (Hab. 2:4). Noteworthy verses in the New Testament are: "The apostles said unto the Lord, 'Increase our faith'" (Luke 17:5); "And His name through faith in His name hath made this man strong, whom ye see and know" (Acts 3:16); "Therein is the righteousness of God revealed from faith to faith" (Rom. 1:17); "Do we then make void the law through faith? God forbid: yea, we establish the law" (Ibid., 3:31); "Hast thou faith? Have it to thyself before God" (Ibid., 14:22).

"Though I have all faith, so that I could remove mountains, and have not charity [love], I am nothing" (1 Cor. 13:2);

"For we walk by faith, not by sight" (2 Cor. 5:7); "Faith which worketh by love" (Gal. 5:6); "Till we all come in the

---

*The word "faith" is used only two times, while "faithful," "faithfully," and "faithfulness" make up the other twenty-six.

**It's interesting to note that nowhere in the book of John is the word "faith" used.

unity of the faith" (Eph. 4:13); "Putting on the breastplate of faith and love" (1 Thess. 5:8); "Fight the good fight of faith" (1 Tim. 6:12); and, "What doth it profit, my brethren, though a man say he hath faith, and have not works? Can faith save him?" (James 2:14).

What exactly does faith *consist of*? Hebrews 11:1 states that, "faith is the substance of things hoped for, the evidence of things not seen." I believe that faith is made up of two important ingredients:

1. "The substance of things hoped for." In other words, you have to first want it to be true. When I first read the Bible, I thought all the stories and promises were wonderful, but my heart sank because I believed they were just fairy tales (or even worse, I thought the Bible might be true and I knew I didn't believe it). But down deep within my heart I decided that I *wanted* it to be true nevertheless.

2. "The evidence of things not seen." From personal experience, I believe that once a person chooses to hope in God, He will then supply evidence of His existence (e.g., the happening of events that are not merely coincidental; the unexpected fulfillment of secret desires; prayers undeniably answered; bona fide miracles; etc.).

Finally, Paul wrote, "We are bound to thank God always for you, brethren, as it is meet [fitting], because that your faith groweth exceedingly" (2 Thess. 1:3). Though "God hath dealt to every man the measure of faith" (Rom. 12:3), it is not a finite amount. Just as the Lord's universe is endless, there is no limit to how much our faith can expand.

For further inquiries,
please send a self-addressed, stamped envelope to:

Sherwood Jansen, Esq.
P.O. Box 27610
San Francisco, CA   94127-0610